Lesson
Enhancers

Lesson Enhancers

Edited and compiled by
Jennifer Jackson and Beth Lefgren

BOOKCRAFT
Salt Lake City, Utah

Library of Congress Catalog Card Number: 89-81704

ISBN 0-88494-723-8

2nd Printing, 1992

Printed in the United States of America

Contents

Preface

No matter where you teach — at church or in the community, in the classroom or at home — this book is for you! You'll find the material in this book perfect for getting the point across.

At times when it seems impossible to find the right words to express particular thoughts or feelings, a good quote can really pin down a message. The quotes found within the covers of this book were selected because they were motivational and thought-provoking as well as concise and comprehensive. You will also find excerpts from scriptures and hymns, quotes which offer added insight and dimension to each subject.

We've been surprised at how versatile quotes can be. Use them in teaching a lesson, in a letter to a special friend, to flavor a talk, or just to ponder. Due to the variety and quality of these quotes, you will find numerous ways to use them.

We also added a bibliography to give you a list of exceptional reference material for any of the topics listed. This can be an excellent tool for additional study.

Use the alphabetized topics at the front to find just the right quote, or just read the book for a spiritual uplift in a quiet moment. No matter how you use *Lesson Enhancers*, we know this is a book you'll refer to again and again.

Activation

Behold, I say unto you, is not a soul at this time as precious unto God as a soul will be at the time of his coming? (Alma 39:17.)

There is none who cannot be converted — or reactivated — if the right person makes the right approach at the right time in the right way with the right spirit. (Spencer W. Kimball, *Ensign*, June 1983, p. 5.)

Usually we must warm our neighbors before we can warn them properly. (Spencer W. Kimball, *Ensign*, July 1985, p. 11.)

We must *care more* for those who seem to *care less* for their faith. (Carlos E. Asay, *Ensign*, October 1986, p. 15.)

The reason, frankly, . . . that so little is happening is that so little is being tried. (Neal A. Maxwell, *Ensign*, May 1982, p. 37.)

If you would convince a man that he does wrong, do right. Men will believe what they see. Let them see. (Henry David Thoreau.)

If you wish your neighbors to see what God is like, let them see what He can make you like. (Charles Kingsley.)

We preach, warning every man, and teaching every man in all wisdom; that we may present every man perfect in Christ Jesus. (Colossians 1:28.)

Motivation [towards activity in the Church] comes when we understand the doctrine. (Jay E. Jensen, *Ensign*, August 1984, p. 20.)

I will heal their backsliding, I will love them freely. (Hosea 14:4.)

Activation requires conversion. (Neal A. Maxwell, *Ensign*, May 1982, p. 37.)

All we like sheep have gone astray; we have turned every one to his own way; and the Lord hath laid on him the iniquity of us all. (Isaiah 53:6.)

Adversity

My people must be tried in all things, that they may be prepared to receive the glory that I have for them. (Doctrine and Covenants 136:31.)

Suffering can make saints of people as they learn patience, long-suffering, and self-mastery. (Spencer W. Kimball, *Tragedy or Destiny?* pp. 2–3.)

Sometimes adversity impels a person to greater heights, and sometimes it provides the opportunity for that person to be a blessing in the lives of others. (Norma H. Hill, *Ensign*, August 1984, p. 64.)

Prosperity is a great teacher; adversity is greater. Possession pampers the mind; privation trains and strengthens it. (William Hazlitt.)

Thou shalt forget thy misery, and remember it as waters that pass away. (Job 11:16.)

We can . . . tell that we are making progress by the attention we get from the adversary. (Spencer W. Kimball, *Ensign*, May 1980, p. 6.)

Difficulties are meant to rouse, not discourage. (William Ellery Channing.)

No pain that we suffer, no trial that we experience is wasted. It ministers to our education, to the development of such qualities as patience, faith, fortitude and humility. (Orson F. Whitney, as quoted in *Improvement Era*, March 1966, p. 211.)

My son, peace be unto thy soul; thine adversity and thine affliction shall be but a small moment. (Doctrine and Covenants 121:7.)

It is trial that proves one thing weak and another strong. . . . A cobweb is as good as the mightiest cable when there is no strain on it. (Henry Ward Beecher.)

> In the furnace God may prove thee,
> Thence to bring thee forth more bright.
> (Thomas Kelly, *Hymns,* no. 43.)

Out of their experience in suffering they bring forth the riches of their sympathy . . . as a blessing to those now in need. (Orson F. Whitney, *Improvement Era,* November 1918, p. 7.)

Anger

Definition: "A feeling that may result from injury, mistreatment, opposition, etc.: it usually shows itself in a desire to hit out at something or someone else." (*Webster's New World Dictionary of the American Language*, p. 56.)

Whenever you get red in the face, whenever you raise your voice, whenever you get "hot under the collar," . . . then know that the Spirit of God is leaving you and the spirit of Satan is beginning to take over. (Theodore M. Burton, *Ensign*, November 1974, p. 56.)

Anger does not contribute to good. It is a destroyer, not a builder. (ElRay L. Christiansen, *Ensign*, June 1971, p. 37.)

A man's disposition is never well known till he be crossed. (Francis Bacon.)

Anger shows a lack of self-control and an inability to relate in a righteous way to others. (L. Lionel Kendrick, *Ensign*, November 1988, p. 24.)

He that is slow to wrath is of great understanding. (Proverbs 14:29.)

The greatest remedy for anger is delay. (Seneca.)

People who fly into a rage always make a bad landing. (Will Rogers.)

He who conquers his wrath overcomes his greatest enemy. (Publilius Syrus.)

For every minute you are angry you lose sixty seconds of happiness. (Ralph Waldo Emerson.)

Appearance

Abstain from all appearance of evil. (1 Thessalonians 5:22.)

Better to look like what you are and be what you ought to be. (Elaine Cannon, *Heart to Heart*, p. 72.)

The way to gain a good reputation is to endeavor to be what you desire to appear. (Socrates.)

To those who would say, "It's what you really are inside that counts, not the length of the hair or beard," I would say, "If this is true and I agree it is, why run the risk of looking like something you're not?" (Marvin J. Ashton, *Ensign*, November 1976, p. 84.)

Associate with men of good quality if you esteem your own reputation; it is better to be alone than in bad company. (George Washington.)

Tell me what company thou keep'st, and I'll tell thee what thou art. (Miguel de Cervantes.)

Look not on his countenance, or on the height of his stature; . . . for the Lord seeth not as man seeth; for man looketh on the outward appearance, but the Lord looketh on the heart. (1 Samuel 16:7.)

You can't judge a horse by the harness. (Proverb.)

Judge not according to the appearance, but judge righteous judgment. (John 7:24.)

Attitude

Definition: "A manner of acting, feeling, or thinking that shows one's disposition or opinion." (*Webster's New World Dictionary of the American Language*, p. 95.)

Let us cheerfully do all things that lie in our power; and then may we stand still, with the utmost assurance, to see the salvation of God, and for his arm to be revealed. (Doctrine and Covenants 123:17.)

Nothing great was ever achieved without enthusiasm. (Ralph Waldo Emerson.)

And they did submit cheerfully and with patience to all the will of the Lord. (Mosiah 24:15.)

I have come to see that if we complain about life, it is because we are thinking only of ourselves. (Gordon B. Hinckley, *Ensign*, August 1982, p. 5.)

It is so difficult to carry our cross and grudges, too. (Neal A. Maxwell, *Ensign*, May 1982, p. 38.)

A merry heart doeth good like a medicine: but a broken spirit drieth the bones. (Proverbs 17:22.)

A burden becomes light which is cheerfully borne. (Ovid.)

Poverty consists in feeling poor. (Ralph Waldo Emerson.)

To be seventy years young is, sometimes, far more cheerful and hopeful than to be forty years old. (Oliver Wendell Holmes.)

If wrinkles must be written upon our brow, let them not grow on the heart. (James A. Garfield.)

Baptism

Definition of the word *baptize:* "To immerse in water . . . to cleanse; purify." (*The American Heritage Dictionary*, p. 57.)

For the gate by which ye should enter is repentance and baptism by water. (2 Nephi 31:17.)

Baptism is the beginning of a new life for each one of us, a life of purpose. (Dwan J. Young, *Ensign*, November 1984, p. 95.)

Baptism is not optional if one wishes the fulness of salvation. (LDS Bible Dictionary, p. 619.)

Baptism is a sign to God, to angels, and to heaven that we do the will of God. (Joseph Smith, *History of the Church*, 4:555.)

> We, who know thy great salvation,
> Are baptized beneath the wave.
> (John Fellows, *Hymns*, no. 234.)

For as many of you as have been baptized into Christ have put on Christ. (Galatians 3:27.)

When we witness our *willingness* to take upon us the name of Jesus Christ, we are signifying our commitment to do all that we can to achieve eternal life. (Dallin H. Oaks, *Ensign*, May 1985, p. 82.)

See that ye are not baptized unworthily; . . . but see that ye do all things in worthiness, . . . and if ye do this, and endure to the end, ye will in nowise be cast out. (Mormon 9:29.)

The Lord has . . . provided a way for us to renew our baptismal covenants through partaking of the sacrament each week. (L. Tom Perry, *Ensign*, November 1984, p. 19.)

Book of Mormon

We believe the Bible to be the word of God as far as it is translated correctly; we also believe the Book of Mormon to be the word of God. (Articles of Faith 1:8.)

We do not have to prove the Book of Mormon is true. The book is its own proof. All we need to do is read it and declare it! (Ezra Taft Benson, *Ensign*, November 1984, p. 8.)

And again, the elders, priests and teachers of this church shall teach the principles of my gospel, which are in the Bible and the Book of Mormon, in the which is the fulness of the gospel. (Doctrine and Covenants 42:12.)

[The Lord] has . . . placed in our hands the most effective, compelling, and persuasive missionary tool ever given to any people in any age, the name of this tool is the Book of Mormon. (Bruce R. McConkie, Conference Report, April 1961, p. 38.)

The Book of Mormon contains messages that were divinely placed there to show how to correct the influence of false tradition and how to receive a fulness of life. (Richard G. Scott, *Ensign*, November 1988, p. 76.)

Truth shall spring out of the earth; and righteousness shall look down from heaven. (Psalm 85:11.)

Therefore, when ye shall receive this record ye may know that the work of the Father has commenced upon all the face of the land. (Ether 4:17.)

No member of this Church can stand approved in the presence of God who has not seriously and carefully read the Book of Mormon. (Joseph Fielding Smith, Conference Report, October 1961, p. 18.)

If we will daily sup from [the] pages [of the Book of Mormon] and abide by its precepts, God will pour out upon each child of Zion and the Church a blessing hitherto unknown. (Ezra Taft Benson, *Ensign*, May 1986, p. 78.)

Character

Our character is but the stamp on our souls of the free choices of good and evil we have made through life. (Cunningham Geikie.)

The measure of a man's real character is what he would do if he knew he would never be found out. (Thomas Macaulay.)

Character is won by hard work. (Delbert L. Stapley, *Relief Society Courses of Study*, 1985, p. 141.)

A man shows his character by what he laughs at. (Johann Wolfgang von Goethe.)

They were men who were true at all times in whatsoever thing they were entrusted. (Alma 53:20.)

Reputation is what men and women think of us. Character is what God and the angels know of us. (Thomas Paine.)

Reputation and character are widely different things. Character lives in a man; reputation outside him. (Josiah Holland.)

If I take care of my character, my reputation will take care of itself. (Dwight L. Moody.)

It is imperative that we do not allow ourselves to be destroyed by the conduct of others. (Marvin J. Ashton, *Ensign*, November 1984, p. 20.)

The integrity of the upright shall guide them. (Proverbs 11:3.)

Children

But little children are holy, being sanctified through the atonement of Jesus Christ. (Doctrine and Covenants 74:7.)

Each time a child is born, the world is renewed in innocence. (Boyd K. Packer, *Ensign*, November 1986, p. 17.)

God sends us children to enlarge our hearts, and to make us unselfish and full of kindly sympathies and affections. (Mary Howitt.)

A child needs a mother more than all the things money can buy. Spending time with your children is the greatest gift of all. (Ezra Taft Benson, *To the Mothers in Zion*, p. 8.)

And when he had said these words, he wept . . . and he took their little children, one by one, and blessed them, and prayed unto the Father for them. (3 Nephi 17:21.)

Bring up your children in the love and fear of the Lord; study their dispositions and their temperaments, and deal with them accordingly. (Brigham Young, as quoted in *Relief Society Courses of Study*, 1985, p. 102.)

Children, obey your parents in all things: for this is well pleasing unto the Lord. (Colossians 3:20.)

Little children do have words given unto them many times, which confound the wise and the learned. (Alma 32:23.)

Children are our most important assets. They need our time. (N. Eldon Tanner, *Ensign*, June 1977, p. 5.)

Make time to teach your children the gospel and principles of gospel living when they are young. (Ezra Taft Benson, *Ensign*, November 1981, p. 106.)

Choice and Accountability

Definitions of the words *choice* and *accountability:* "The right or power to choose," "responsibility for one's own actions, for which one must be called to account." (*Webster's New World Dictionary of the American Language,* pp. 256, 1240.)

Say unto this people: Choose ye this day, to serve the Lord God who made you. (Moses 6:33.)

Decisions do determine destiny. (Thomas S. Monson, *Ensign,* November 1986, p. 40.)

Our lives are made up of thousands of everyday choices. Over the years these little choices will be bundled together and show clearly what we value. (Boyd K. Packer, *Ensign,* November 1980, p. 21.)

Ponder the path of thy feet, and let all thy ways be established. (Proverbs 4:26.)

No one became thoroughly bad in one step. (Juvenal.)

If we want to meet our own particular destiny, we must be certain we are on the path that will lead us there. (Elaine Cannon, *Heart to Heart,* p. 12.)

Therefore, cheer up your hearts, and remember that ye are free to act for yourselves — to choose the way of everlasting death or the way of eternal life. (2 Nephi 10:23.)

Freedom of choice is more to be treasured than any possession earth can give. (David O. McKay, Conference Report, April 1950, p. 32.)

God hath entrusted me with myself. (Epictetus.)

It is contrary to the order of heaven for any soul to be locked into compulsive, immoral behavior with no way out! (Boyd K. Packer, *Ensign*, November 1986, p. 18.)

That every man may act in doctrine and principle pertaining to futurity, according to the moral agency which I have given unto him, that every man may be accountable for his own sins in the day of judgment. (Doctrine and Covenants 101:78.)

If you have not chosen the kingdom of God first, it will in the end make no difference what you have chosen instead. (William Law.)

Communication

Let your speech be alway with grace, seasoned with salt, that ye may know how ye ought to answer every man. (Colossians 4:6.)

Effective communication must include positive verbal exchanges—happy talk as well as pleasant negotiation. It means dealing with feelings in open and honest but non-attacking ways. (Victor B. Cline, *How to Make Your Child a Winner*, p. 67.)

Pleasant words are as an honeycomb, sweet to the soul, and health to the bones. (Proverbs 16:24.)

Without effective communication, we fail to share ourselves. (Suzanne L. Hansen, *Working and Winning with Kids*, p. 42.)

Lift up your voices unto this people; speak the thoughts that I shall put into your hearts, and you shall not be confounded before men. (Doctrine and Covenants 100:5.)

Silence and modesty are very valuable qualities in conversation. (Michel de Montaigne.)

A soft answer turneth away wrath: but grievous words stir up anger. (Proverbs 15:1.)

Quiet talk is the language of love. It is the language of peace. It is the language of God. (Gordon B. Hinckley, *Relief Society Personal Study Guide*, 1988, p. 181.)

As children of our Heavenly Father we can glorify him and his Son Jesus Christ with better words of love and appreciation . . . and with a desire to communicate in a divine way. (Charles A. Didier, *Ensign*, November 1979, p. 26.)

Contention

For where envying and strife is, there is confusion and every evil work. (James 3:16.)

Where contention prevails, there can be no united effort in any purposeful direction. (Marvin J. Ashton, *Ensign*, November 1987, p. 22.)

Evil forces are working relentlessly to have us bring contention into our homes over any issue and threaten our happiness, our peace, and our love for each other. (Ardeth G. Kapp, *Ensign*, November 1984, p. 97.)

Do all things without murmurings and disputings. (Philippians 2:14.)

Quarrels would not last long if the fault was only on one side. (La Rochefoucauld.)

When one will not, two cannot quarrel. (Proverb.)

Only by pride cometh contention. (Proverbs 13:10.)

The peaceful life can best be attained not by those who speak with a voice of "great tumultuous noise" but by those who follow the Savior's example and speak with "a still voice of perfect mildness." (Marvin J. Ashton, *Ensign*, May 1978, p. 9.)

It is when we raise our voices that tiny mole hills of difference become mountains of conflict. (Gordon B. Hinckley, *Relief Society Personal Study Guide*, 1988, p. 181.)

Courage

Courage, not compromise, brings the smile of God's approval. (Thomas S. Monson, *Ensign*, November 1986, p. 41.)

The hero is no braver than an ordinary man, but he is braver five minutes longer. (Ralph Waldo Emerson.)

The courage we desire and prize is not the courage to die decently, but to live manfully. (Thomas Carlyle.)

Conscience is at the root of all true courage. If a man would be brave, let him obey his conscience. (James Freeman Clark.)

Courage consists not in blindly overlooking danger, but in meeting it with the eyes open. (Jean Paul Richter.)

Courage and perseverance have a magical talisman, before which difficulties disappear and obstacles vanish into air. (John Quincy Adams.)

We gain courage by the realization that we have a lot going for us. (Derek A. Cuthbert, *New Era*, November 1985, p. 46.)

Be strong and of a good courage, fear not, nor be afraid of them: for the Lord thy God, he it is that doth go with thee. (Deuteronomy 31:6.)

Keep your fears to yourself but share your courage with others. (Robert Louis Stevenson.)

Whoever is brave is a man of great soul. (Marcus Cicero.)

Deal courageously, and the Lord shall be with the good. (2 Chronicles 19:11.)

Criticism

Definition: "The general term for finding fault with or disapproving of a person or thing." (*Webster's New World Dictionary of the American Language*, p. 339.)

Cease to contend one with another; cease to speak evil one of another. (Doctrine and Covenants 136:23.)

We keep the faults of others before our eyes; our own behind our backs. (Seneca.)

Too often it is easier to criticize, to point out the faults, than to praise or give love. (Paul H. Dunn, *Relief Society Courses of Study*, 1985, p. 122.)

It is much easier to be critical than to be correct. (Benjamin Disraeli.)

Thou shalt be favored of the Lord, because thou hast not murmured. (1 Nephi 3:6.)

The imperfections of others never release us from the need to work on our own shortcomings. (Neal A. Maxwell, *Ensign*, May 1982, p. 39.)

How seldom we weigh our neighbor in the same balance as ourselves. (Thomas à Kempis.)

It is so easy to find fault, and to resist doing so requires much of discipline. (Gordon B. Hinckley, *Ensign*, May 1982, p. 46.)

Criticism is futile because it puts a man on the defensive, and usually makes him strive to justify himself. (Dale Carnegie, *How to Win Friends and Influence People*, p. 21.)

Reproving betimes with sharpness, when moved upon by the Holy Ghost; and then showing forth afterwards an increase of love toward him whom thou hast reproved, lest he esteem thee to be his enemy. (Doctrine and Covenants 121:43.)

Let us be grateful for the small strides that we and others make, rather than rejoice in the shortfalls. (Neal A. Maxwell, *Ensign*, May 1982, p. 39.)

Death

Thou know'st 'tis common—all that lives must die,
Passing through nature to eternity.
(William Shakespeare, Hamlet 1.2.72.)

Then shall the dust return to the earth as it was: and the spirit shall return unto God who gave it. (Ecclesiastes 12:7.)

It is vital to come to an understanding that death is not the end but a new beginning. (Derek A. Cuthbert, *New Era*, November 1985, p. 48.)

Death? Translated into the heavenly tongue, that word means life. (Henry Ward Beecher.)

To obtain a resurrection with a celestial, exalted body is the center point of hope in the gospel of Jesus Christ. (LDS Bible Dictionary, p. 761.)

Why should it be thought a thing incredible with you, that God should raise the dead? (Acts 26:8.)

We need not doubt the reality of the Resurrection simply because we do not understand it. (Neal A. Maxwell, *Ensign*, June 1984, p. 71.)

They are not dead, but have only finished the journey which it is necessary for every one of us to take. (Antiphanes.)

The grave must deliver up its captive bodies, and the bodies and the spirits of men will be restored one to the other; and it is by the power of the resurrection of the Holy One of Israel. (2 Nephi 9:12.)

It is impossible that anything so natural, so necessary, and so universal as death should ever have been designed as an evil to mankind. (Jonathan Swift.)

Death is a blessing, for it opens the way to the faithful for further progression on the way to eternal life. (Roy W. Doxey, *The Doctrine and Covenants Speaks,* 1:495.)

For if we have been planted together in the likeness of his death, we shall be also in the likeness of his resurrection. (Romans 6:5.)

Depression

Definition: "An emotional condition characterized by discouragement, a feeling of inadequacy, etc." (*Webster's New World Dictionary of the American Language*, p. 395.)

We can rise above the enemies of despair, depression, discouragement, and despondency by remembering that God provides righteous alternatives. (Ezra Taft Benson, *Ensign*, October 1986, p. 5.)

Now when our hearts were depressed . . . the Lord comforted us. (Alma 26:27.)

Save me, O God; for the waters are come in unto my soul. . . . I am weary of my crying: my throat is dried: mine eyes fail while I wait for my God. (Psalm 69:1, 3.)

I must lose myself in action, lest I wither in despair. (Alfred, Lord Tennyson.)

Yea, though I walk through the valley of the shadow of death, I will fear no evil: for thou art with me; thy rod and thy staff they comfort me. (Psalm 23:4.)

People are lonely because they build walls instead of bridges. (Joseph Fort Newton.)

We are troubled on every side, yet not distressed; we are perplexed, but not in despair; persecuted, but not forsaken; cast down, but not destroyed. (2 Corinthians 4:8–9.)

Divine Nature

I have said, Ye are gods; and all of you are children of the most High. (Psalm 82:6.)

If we understand our relationship to God our Father, we cannot possibly be irreverent toward ourselves. (Marion G. Romney, *Ensign*, September 1982, p. 4.)

It takes solitude, under the stars, for us to be reminded of our eternal origin and our far destiny. (Archibald Rutledge.)

What is man, that thou art mindful of him? . . . For thou hast made him a little lower than the angels. (Psalm 8:4–5.)

What we are is God's gift to us. What we become is our gift to God. (Louis Nizer.)

Every individual has a place to fill in the world, and is important, in some respect, whether he chooses to be so or not. (Nathaniel Hawthorne.)

You . . . are *everything;* you are *why* the heavens were created. (Ted E. Brewerton, *Ensign*, November 1986, p. 30.)

It is in men as in soils, where sometimes there is a vein of gold which the owner knows not of. (Jonathan Swift.)

What a man believes about immortality will color his thinking in every area of life. (John Sutherland Bonnell.)

What a difference it would make if we really sensed our divine relationship to God, . . . our relationship to Jesus Christ, . . . and our relationship to each other. (Harold B. Lee, *Relief Society Personal Study Guide*, 1988, p. 244.)

Exaltation

Definition of the word *exalt:* "To raise in status, dignity, power, honor, wealth, etc.: to glorify: to fill with joy." (*Webster's New World Dictionary of the American Language*, p. 504.)

For if you will that I give unto you a place in the celestial world, you must prepare yourselves by doing the things which I have commanded you and required of you. (Doctrine and Covenants 78:7.)

Our exaltation, our future glory depends entirely upon our obedience to law. (George Q. Cannon, Conference Report, April 1900, p. 54.)

Mere *belief* in Christ is not sufficient, but *obedience to his laws* is *essential* to salvation and exaltation. (N. Eldon Tanner, *Ensign*, April 1982, p. 4.)

And then, if thou endure it well, God shall exalt thee on high; thou shalt triumph over all thy foes. (Doctrine and Covenants 121:8.)

All men may become what He is if they will pay the price. (Melvin J. Ballard, *The Three Degrees of Glory*, p. 9.)

Then shall the righteous shine forth as the sun in the kingdom of their Father. (Matthew 13:43.)

If we refrain from evil acts, we have clean hands. If we refrain from forbidden thoughts, we have pure hearts. Those who would ascend and stand in the ultimate holy place must have both. (Dallin H. Oaks, *Ensign*, June 1986, p. 66.)

A man may receive the priesthood and all its privileges and blessings, but until he learns to overcome the flesh . . . [and] his disposition to indulge in the things God has forbidden, he cannot come into the celestial kingdom of God. (Melvin J. Ballard, *The Three Degrees of Glory*, p. 11.)

For he who is not able to abide the law of a celestial kingdom cannot abide a celestial glory. (Doctrine and Covenants 88:22.)

The celestial kingdom will be made up of people who are ordinary in an earthly sense but extraordinary in a spiritual sense. (Anita Canfield, *The Young Woman and Her Self-Esteem*, p. 4.)

He that overcometh shall inherit all things; and I will be his God, and he shall be my son. (Revelation 21:7.)

Example

For I have given you an example, that ye should do as I have done to you. (John 13:15.)

There is no power on earth that can neutralize the influence of a high, pure, simple, and useful life. (Booker T. Washington.)

One of the most important ways we can follow . . . is to emulate the prophet's example. ("Teaching Children to Follow the Prophet," *Ensign*, March 1989, p. 55.)

Show forth good examples unto them in me, and I will make an instrument of thee in my hands unto the salvation of many souls. (Alma 17:11.)

If you try to improve one person by being a good example, you're improving two. If you try to improve someone without being a good example, you won't improve anybody. (James Thorn.)

Only prophets can lead us safely through this life and back into the presence of our Heavenly Father. ("Teaching Children to Follow the Prophet," *Ensign*, March 1989, p. 55.)

A child went forth and became what he saw. (Walt Whitman.)

He was of that good kind that you are likely to forget while they are present, but remember distinctly after they are gone. (O. Henry.)

If you would lift me you must be on higher ground. (Ralph Waldo Emerson.)

> Each life that touches ours for good
> Reflects thine own great mercy, Lord.
> (Karen Lynn Davidson, *Hymns,* no. 293.)

Let your light so shine before this people, that they may see your good works and glorify your Father who is in heaven. (3 Nephi 12:16.)

Faith

Now faith is the substance of things hoped for, the evidence of things not seen. (Hebrews 11:1.)

Faith is the foundation upon which a godlike character is built. (Ezra Taft Benson, *Ensign*, November 1986, p. 45.)

Without faith a man can do nothing; with it all things are possible. (Sir William Osler.)

Yea, and how is it that ye have forgotten that the Lord is able to do all things according to his will, for the children of men, if it so be that they exercise faith in him? Wherefore, let us be faithful to him. (1 Nephi 7:12.)

We're not going to survive in this world, temporally or spiritually, without increased faith in the Lord. (A. Theodore Tuttle, *Ensign*, November 1986, p. 73.)

What is faith unless it is to believe what you do not see? (Augustine.)

According to your faith be it unto you. (Matthew 9:29.)

Pin not your faith on another's sleeve. (Proverb.)

If ye will have faith in me ye shall have power to do whatsoever thing is expedient in me. (Moroni 7:33.)

As one studies by faith, his concepts of God and eternity are enlarged, and his power to do good is increased. (Roy W. Doxey, *The Doctrine and Covenants Speaks*, 2:410.)

Family

The patterns we set in our homes and the values we develop there, whether they be good or bad, almost cannot be overcome. (Dean L. Larsen, *Ensign*, May 1983, p. 33.)

Honour thy father and mother; (which is the first commandment with promise;) that it may be well with thee, and thou mayest live long on the earth. (Ephesians 6:2–3.)

A home is not a home in the eye of the gospel, unless there dwell perfect confidence and love between the husband and the wife. (Joseph F. Smith, *Gospel Doctrine*, p. 302.)

He [Satan] knows that if he can cause parents to quarrel with each other, their children may well follow the example. (H. Burke Peterson, *Ensign*, January 1973, p. 114.)

Heaven at home is a pleasant possibility when everybody tries. (Elaine Cannon, *Heart to Heart*, p. 22.)

A happy family is but an earlier heaven. (Bowring.)

Like iron links in a chain, [family home evening] will bind a family together, in love, pride, tradition, strength, and loyalty. (Ezra Taft Benson, *Ensign*, November 1982, p. 60.)

Family pride grows out of family traditions . . . out of doing things together. (Paul H. Dunn, *Relief Society Courses of Study*, 1985, p. 133.)

A man cannot leave a better legacy to the world than a well-educated family. (Thomas Scott.)

We have been so anxious to give our children what we didn't have that we have neglected to give them what we did have. (Anonymous.)

The time will come when only those who believe deeply and actively in the family will be able to preserve their families in the midst of the gathering evil around us. (Spencer W. Kimball, *Ensign*, November 1980, p. 4.)

Fasting

I humbled my soul with fasting. (Psalm 35:13.)

Fasting and prayer and pondering and visions and revelations prepare men for the ministry, and it was no different, except in degree, where the preparation of the Lord Jesus was concerned. (Bruce R. McConkie, *The Mortal Messiah*, 1:410.)

Is not this the fast that I have chosen? to loose the bands of wickedness, to undo the heavy burdens, and to let the oppressed go free, and that ye break every yoke? (Isaiah 58:6.)

The most perfect fasting is done when the desire to pray is so great that there is no thought nor time to eat nor concern oneself with the needs of the body. . . . We should not have to be forced into feeling the need for fasting and prayer. (Max B. Skousen, *How to Pray and Stay Awake*, p. 118.)

I have known children to cry for something to eat on fast day. . . . The compulsion [to fast] engenders a spirit of rebellion in them, rather than a love for the Lord and their fellows. Better teach them the principle . . . than to so compel them. (Joseph F. Smith, *Gospel Doctrine*, p. 244.)

Appear not unto men to fast, but unto thy Father which is in secret: and thy Father, which seeth in secret, shall reward thee openly. (Matthew 6:18.)

Failing to fast is a sin. (Spencer W. Kimball, *The Miracle of Forgiveness*, p. 98.)

And on this day thou shalt do none other thing, only let thy food be prepared with singleness of heart that thy fasting may be perfect, or, in other words, that thy joy may be full. (Doctrine and Covenants 59:13.)

Have you some besetting weakness, some sinful indulgence that you have vainly tried to overcome? . . . Your sin may be of a kind that goeth out only through prayer and fasting. (James E. Talmage, *Jesus the Christ*, p. 395.)

Fathers

Hear, ye children, the instruction of a father, and attend to know understanding. (Proverbs 4:1.)

The father is the head of every home, and even though the mother may be just as brilliant or more so, the father has been set apart by the Lord to look after his family. (Spencer W. Kimball, *The Teachings of Spencer W. Kimball*, p. 344.)

We all know fatherhood is not an easy assignment, but it ranks among the most imperative ever given. (Jeffrey R. Holland, *Ensign*, May 1983, p. 38.)

A wise bishop will recognize each boy's father as his most important helper. (Victor L. Brown, *Ensign*, May 1982, p. 35.)

Fathers, draw close to your children. . . . This means giving a father's most valuable commodity — time! (A. Theodore Tuttle, *Ensign*, January 1974, p. 67.)

The presence of a firm, loving father in the home is far more likely to produce responsible, law-abiding children. (James E. Faust, *Ensign*, May 1983, p. 40.)

What a father says to his children is not heard by the world, but it will be heard by posterity. (Jean Paul Richter.)

When fathers are tongue-tied religiously, need they wonder if their children's hearts remain sin-tied? (Charles H. Spurgeon.)

And ye fathers, provoke not your children to wrath: but bring them up in the nurture and admonition of the Lord. (Ephesians 6:4.)

Certainly if fathers are to be respected, they must merit respect —if they are to be loved, they must be consistent, lovable, understanding, and kind, and they must honor their priesthood. (Spencer W. Kimball, *Ensign*, January 1975, p. 5.)

Man, as well as woman, has obligations to learn the difficult art of fatherhood in homemaking. This is not a task just for the woman. (G. Homer Durham, *Woman*, p. 36.)

Fear

For God hath not given us the spirit of fear; but of power, and of love, and of a sound mind. (2 Timothy 1:7.)

We have no need to fear. We have no need to worry. We have no need to speculate. Our imperative need is to be found doing our duty individually in callings which have come to us. (Gordon B. Hinckley, *Ensign*, May 1983, p. 6.)

In God I have put my trust; I will not fear what flesh can do unto me. (Psalm 56:4.)

Nothing in life is to be feared. It is only to be understood. (Marie Curie.)

The greatest mistake you can make in life is to be continually fearing you will make one. (Elbert Hubbard.)

There is no fear in love; but perfect love casteth out fear. (1 John 4:18.)

To return good for evil not only overcomes fear but also overcomes enmity. (Derek A. Cuthbert, *New Era*, November 1985, p. 44.)

If ye are prepared ye shall not fear. (Doctrine and Covenants 38:30.)

We need not fear the future if we hold fast to revealed principles. (Gordon B. Hinckley, *Ensign*, May 1983, p. 7.)

Therefore, whosoever belongeth to my church need not fear, for such shall inherit the kingdom of heaven. (Doctrine and Covenants 10:55.)

Following Christ

I testify to you that there is no greater, more thrilling, and more soul-ennobling challenge than to try to learn of Christ and walk in His steps. (Ezra Taft Benson, *Relief Society Course of Study*, 1987, p. 137.)

Yea, thus we see that the gate of heaven is open unto all, even to those who will believe on the name of Jesus Christ. (Helaman 3:28.)

The cultivation of Christlike qualities is a demanding and relentless task—it is not for the seasonal worker. (Spencer W. Kimball, *Relief Society Course of Study*, 1987, p. 126.)

When a person truly loves God with everything that is in him, it is not a hard thing to live with an eye that is single to the glory of Christ. (Max B. Skousen, *How to Pray and Stay Awake*, p. 135.)

Internalizing of the teachings of the Savior in the heart of any boy can become a protection from the evils of the world. (Victor L. Brown, *Ensign*, May 1982, p. 36.)

Yea, blessed is this people who are willing to bear my name. (Mosiah 26:18.)

Try the ways of being good, and you will fail; but try the way of Christ and you will succeed. (Matthew Arnold.)

If our distance from him increases, it is we who have moved and not the Lord. (Spencer W. Kimball, *Faith Precedes the Miracle*, p. 208.)

Take my yoke upon you, and learn of me; . . . and ye shall find rest unto your souls. (Matthew 11:29.)

If we are to walk in the steps of the Savior, we cannot do it without personal sacrifice and sincere involvement. (J. Richard Clarke, *Ensign*, November 1981, p. 82.)

One who has a profound reverence for the Lord loves him, trusts in him, prays to him, relies upon him, and is inspired by him. (Marion G. Romney, *Ensign*, July 1983, p. 5.)

Every character has an inward spring; let Christ be that spring. Every action has a keynote; let Christ be that note, to which your whole life is attuned. (Henry Drummond.)

Forgiveness

Definition of the word *forgive:* "To give up resentment against or the desire to punish; to stop being angry with; to give up all claim to punish or exact a penalty for." (*Webster's New World Dictionary of the American Language*, p. 568.)

Behold, he who has repented of his sins, the same is forgiven, and I, the Lord, remember them no more. (Doctrine and Covenants 58:42.)

Forgiveness is powerful spiritual medicine. (Boyd K. Packer, *Ensign*, November 1987, p. 18.)

For if ye forgive men their trespasses, your heavenly Father will also forgive you. (Matthew 6:14.)

God cannot deal with us on the basis of forgiveness while we are harboring ill-will against those who have wronged us. (Max B. Skousen, *How to Pray and Stay Awake*, p. 132.)

And be ye kind one to another, tenderhearted, forgiving one another, even as God for Christ's sake hath forgiven you. (Ephesians 4:32.)

"I can forgive, but I cannot forget," is only another way of saying, "I cannot forgive." (Henry Ward Beecher.)

The Lord's forgiveness is withheld until the person can also forgive his fellow men. (Roy W. Doxey, *The Doctrine and Covenants Speaks*, 1:505.)

It becomes us . . . to reach out with a spirit of forgiveness . . . toward those whom we have felt may have wronged us. (Gordon B. Hinckley, *Ensign*, November 1980, p. 61.)

Come now, and let us reason together, saith the Lord: though your sins be as scarlet, they shall be as white as snow; though they be red like crimson, they shall be as wool. (Isaiah 1:18.)

Free Agency

And I gave unto them their knowledge, in the day I created them; and in the Garden of Eden, gave I unto man his agency. (Moses 7:32.)

Let us . . . understand that God in his love for us will not take away from us the dignity of the individual—our free agency. (F. Enzio Busche, *Ensign*, January 1982, p. 52.)

We are born subjects, and to obey God is perfect liberty. He that does this shall be free, safe, and happy. (Seneca.)

He that is good is free, though he be a slave; he that is evil is a slave, though he be a king. (Augustine.)

No man is free who cannot command himself. (Seneca.)

Therefore, cheer up your hearts, and remember that ye are free to act for yourselves—to choose the way of everlasting death or the way of eternal life. (2 Nephi 10:23.)

May you realize that in you is the control of your life and what you are going to be, what you are going to do. (Spencer W. Kimball, *Ensign*, November 1978, p. 105.)

The God who gave us life, gave us liberty at the same time. (Thomas Jefferson.)

You are the author of your own book of Acts, writer of your script, star of your season. (Elaine Cannon, *Heart to Heart*, p. 49.)

Wherefore, men . . . are free to choose liberty and eternal life, through the great Mediator of all men, or to choose captivity and death, according to the captivity and power of the devil. (2 Nephi 2:27.)

God never planted his Spirit, his truth in the hearts of men from the point of a bayonet. (J. Reuben Clark, Conference Report, April 1957, p. 51.)

If you have not chosen the Kingdom of God first, it will in the end make no difference what you have chosen instead. (William Law.)

Next to the bestowal of life itself, the right to direct that life is God's greatest gift to man. (David O. McKay, *Improvement Era*, February 1962, p. 86.)

Friendship

A friend loveth at all times, and a brother is born for adversity. (Proverbs 17:17.)

The fellowship of true friends who can hear you out, share your joys, help carry your burdens, and correctly counsel you is priceless. (Ezra Taft Benson, *Ensign*, October 1986, p. 4.)

> What greater gift dost thou bestow
> What greater goodness can we know
> Than Christlike friends, whose gentle ways
> Strengthen our faith, enrich our days.
> (Karen Lynn Davidson, *Hymns*, no. 293.)

A true friend unbosoms freely, advises justly, assists readily, adventures boldly, takes all patiently, defends courageously, and continues a friend unchangeably. (William Penn.)

Thy friends do stand by thee, and they shall hail thee again with warm hearts and friendly hands. (Doctrine and Covenants 121:9.)

If a loving and caring person steps forward at the time of crisis and offers honest assistance, the relationship is enhanced. It becomes firm and persuasive as willing sacrifices are made and as personal bonds of friendship are established. (Carlos E. Asay, *Ensign*, October 1986, p. 15.)

Friendship consists in forgetting what one gives and remembering what one receives. (Alexandre Dumas.)

A true friend is one who not only is willing to love us the way we are, but is able to leave us better than he found us. (Marvin J. Ashton, *Ensign*, September 1982, p. 73.)

The only way to have a friend is to be one. (Ralph Waldo Emerson.)

Greater love hath no man than this, that a man lay down his life for his friends. (John 15:13.)

Goals

A prerequisite for "doing" is goal setting. (Marvin J. Ashton, *Ensign*, May 1983, p. 31.)

A man who does not think and plan long ahead will find trouble right at his door. (Confucius.)

Ah, but a man's reach should exceed his grasp, or what's a heaven for? (Robert Browning.)

I press toward the mark for the prize of the high calling of God in Christ Jesus. (Philippians 3:14.)

The great thing in this world is not so much where we stand, as in what direction we are moving. (Oliver Wendell Holmes.)

But seek ye first the kingdom of God and his righteousness, and all these things shall be added unto you. (3 Nephi 13:33.)

Eternal things are always done in the process of time. . . . Direction is initially more important than speed. (Neal A. Maxwell, *Of One Heart*, p. 35.)

But before ye seek for riches, seek ye for the kingdom of God. (Jacob 2:18.)

Remember, the kingdom of God, the power of God, the glory of God should be man's most cherished and important blessings and goals in this life. (Bernard P. Brockbank, *Ensign*, November 1979, p. 58.)

The journey of a thousand miles begins with one step. (Lao-tse.)

Beware of what you want, for you will get it. (Ralph Waldo Emerson.)

Goals without action equal nothing. (Anita Canfield, *The Young Woman and Her Self-Esteem*, p. 25.)

Keep my commandments, and seek to bring forth and establish the cause of Zion. (Doctrine and Covenants 6:6.)

Gossip

The words of a talebearer are as wounds, and they go down into the innermost parts of the belly. (Proverbs 18:8.)

There would not be so many open mouths if there were not so many open ears. (John Hall.)

Gossip is the worst form of judging. (N. Eldon Tanner, *Ensign*, July 1972, p. 35.)

Gossip bespeaks either a vacant mind or one that entertains jealousy or envy. (David O. McKay, *Improvement Era*, December 1954, p. 931.)

When you hear stories, be wise. Unless you are in all the interviews, and hear all the evidence, you are not in a position to really know. Be careful, lest you jump to a confusion. (Boyd K. Packer, *Ensign*, May 1979, p. 80.)

Habit

Habits are at first cobwebs, then cables. (Spanish Proverb.)

The chains of habit are generally too small to be felt until they are too strong to be broken. (Samuel Johnson.)

It is easier to suppress the first desire than to satisfy all that follow it. (Benjamin Franklin.)

The mind is slow in unlearning what it has been long in learning. (Seneca.)

His own iniquities shall take the wicked himself, and he shall be holden with the cords of his sins. (Proverbs 5:22.)

Happiness

True happiness is to understand our duties toward God and man; to enjoy the present, without anxious dependence upon the future; not to amuse ourselves with either hopes or fears, but to rest satisfied with what we have . . . for he that is so wants nothing. (Seneca.)

We have a moral obligation to exercise our personal capabilities of mind, muscle, and spirit in a way that will return to the Lord . . . the fruits of our best efforts. To do less is to live our lives unfulfilled. (J. Richard Clarke, *Ensign*, May 1982, p. 77.)

A man must seek his happiness and inward peace from objects which cannot be taken away from him. (Wilhelm von Humboldt.)

Behold, I say unto you, wickedness never was happiness. (Alma 41:10.)

Happy is the individual whose personal code of honor dictates behavior consistent with the eternal principles of growth. (Dallin H. Oaks, *Relief Society Courses of Study*, 1985, p. 145.)

I would desire that ye should consider on the blessed and happy state of those that keep the commandments of God. . . . And if they hold out faithful to the end they are received into heaven, that thereby they may dwell with God in a state of never-ending happiness. (Mosiah 2:41.)

Most folks are about as happy as they make up their minds to be. (Abraham Lincoln.)

We have to learn how to make our heaven before we can live in it. (Elaine Cannon, *Heart to Heart*, p. 52.)

Success is getting what you want; happiness is wanting what you get. (Thomas Kettering.)

Holy Ghost

But the Comforter, which is the Holy Ghost, whom the Father will send in my name, he shall teach you all things, and bring all things to your remembrance, whatsoever I have said unto you. (John 14:26.)

> The Spirit, voice
> Of goodness, whispers to our hearts
> A better choice
> Than evil's anguished cries.
> (Edward L. Hart, *Hymns*, no. 113.)

God does not send thunder if a still, small voice is enough. (Neal A. Maxwell, *Ensign*, November 1976, p. 14.)

The Spirit does not get our attention by shouting or shaking us with a heavy hand. Rather it whispers. It caresses so gently that if we are preoccupied we may not hear it at all. (Boyd K. Packer, *Ensign*, January 1983, p. 53.)

For, behold, the Comforter knoweth all things, and beareth record of the Father and of the Son. (Doctrine and Covenants 42:17.)

With your very being held still, you should listen to the whisperings of the Holy Spirit. You should follow the noble, intuitive feelings planted deep within your soul by Deity in the previous world. (James E. Faust, *Relief Society Course of Study*, 1987, p. 80.)

Ask the Father in my name, in faith believing that you shall receive, and you shall have the Holy Ghost, which manifesteth all things which are expedient unto the children of men. (Doctrine and Covenants 18:18.)

Some answers will come from reading the scriptures, some from hearing speakers. And, occasionally, when it is important, some will come by very direct and powerful inspiration. The promptings will be clear and unmistakable. (Boyd K. Packer, *Ensign*, November 1979, p. 21.)

We cannot neglect, slight, or depart from the spirit, . . . without shearing ourselves of our glory, strength, right and title to his blessings. (Joseph F. Smith, *Improvement Era*, August 1906, p. 813.)

But the fruit of the Spirit is love, joy, peace, longsuffering, gentleness, goodness, faith, meekness, temperance: against such there is no law. (Galatians 5:22–23.)

Honesty

Definition of the word *honest:* "Genuine, having or manifesting integrity and truth." (*The American Heritage Dictionary*, p. 340.)

Provide things honest in the sight of all men. (Romans 12:17.)

Honesty is more than a policy. It is a happy way of life as we deal with our fellowmen, and particularly as we live with ourselves. (Marvin J. Ashton, *Ensign*, May 1982, p. 11.)

Take upon you the name of Christ, and speak the truth in soberness. (Doctrine and Covenants 18:21.)

Honesty is the foundation of a sound character and the keystone of all other virtues. (William Grant Bangerter, *New Era*, September 1979, p. 4.)

He that worketh deceit shall not dwell within my house: he that telleth lies shall not tarry in my sight. (Psalm 101:7.)

He that loseth his honesty hath nothing else to lose. (John Lyly.)

A lie travels round the world while Truth is putting on her boots. (Charles Haddon Spurgeon.)

It often requires more bravery to tell the simple truth than it does to win a battle. (Josh Billings [Henry Wheeler Shaw].)

The mind must not only possess a knowledge of truth, but the soul must revere it, cherish it, love it as a priceless gem; and this human life must be guided and shaped by it in order to fulfill its destiny. (Joseph F. Smith, *Gospel Doctrine*, p. 269.)

Hope

Definition: "To desire something with some confidence of its fulfillment." (*The American Heritage Dictionary*, p. 342.)

How is it that ye can attain unto faith, save ye shall have hope? (Moroni 7:40.)

Hope means we really trust the Lord. (Dwan J. Young, *Ensign*, November 1986, p. 87.)

Everything that is done in this world is done by hope. (Martin Luther.)

And if ye have no hope ye must needs be in despair; and despair cometh because of iniquity. (Moroni 10:22.)

Above the cloud with its shadow is the star with its light. (Victor Hugo.)

Hope is knowing that whatever comes, the Lord can whisper peace. (Dwan J. Young, *Ensign*, November 1986, p. 86.)

Wherefore man must hope, or he cannot receive an inheritance in the place which thou hast prepared. (Ether 12:32.)

We as Latter-day Saints should be the most optimistic and the least pessimistic. (Ezra Taft Benson, *Ensign*, November 1974, p. 65.)

Humility

Be thou humble; and the Lord thy God shall lead thee by the hand, and give thee answer to thy prayers. (Doctrine and Covenants 112:10.)

Humility is the solid foundation of all the virtues. (Confucius.)

And whosoever shall exalt himself shall be abased; and he that shall humble himself shall be exalted. (Matthew 23:12.)

Do you wish people to speak well of you? Don't yourself. (Blaise Pascal.)

Humility is a virtue all preach, none practice, and yet everybody is content to hear. (John Selden.)

If they humble themselves before me, and have faith in me, then will I make weak things become strong unto them. (Ether 12:27.)

Whosoever therefore shall humble himself as this little child, the same is greatest in the kingdom of heaven. (Matthew 18:4.)

Humility is the quality of being teachable, of responding fully to the Lord's will. (Roy W. Doxey, *The Doctrine and Covenants Speaks*, 1:447.)

Humility is the precious, fertile soil of righteous character. (Richard G. Scott, *Ensign*, November 1981, p. 12.)

Without this basic Christian virtue of humility there is neither spiritual progression here nor eternal life hereafter. (Bruce R. McConkie, *Doctrinal New Testament Commentary*, 1:500.)

Humble yourselves in the sight of the Lord, and he shall lift you up. (James 4:10.)

Individual Worth

Definition: "Belief in one's self; self-respect." (*Webster's New World Dictionary of the American Language,* p. 1322.)

Remember the worth of souls is great in the sight of God. (Doctrine and Covenants 18:10.)

Believe in yourself, and what others think won't matter. (Ralph Waldo Emerson.)

I will make a man more precious than fine gold; even a man than the golden wedge of Ophir. (Isaiah 13:12.)

You . . . are *everything;* you are *why* the heavens were created. (Ted E. Brewerton, *Ensign,* November 1986, p. 30.)

[Finding one's identity] comes only through knowledge of and obedience to the commandments. (Victor L. Brown, *Ensign,* May 1983, p. 60.)

And the great God has had mercy upon us, and made these things known unto us that we might not perish; yea, and he has made these things known unto us beforehand, because he loveth our souls as well as he loveth our children. (Alma 24:14.)

When we see one devoid of respect for himself . . . then certainly we are witnessing the frightening aspect of one over whom Satan has achieved a victory. (Harold B. Lee, *Relief Society Personal Study Guide,* 1988, p. 243.)

We should teach, particularly ourselves, that nobody is a nobody. We are someone, and with God's help we can accomplish all things. (Marvin J. Ashton, *Ensign,* September 1982, p. 74.)

Integrity

Definition: "A quality or state of being of sound moral principle; uprightness, honesty, and sincerity." (*Webster's New World Dictionary of the American Language*, p. 759.)

The just man walketh in his integrity: his children are blessed after him. (Proverbs 20:7.)

To me the highest thing, after God, is my honor. (Ludwig van Beethoven.)

Do that which you judge to be beautiful and honest, though you should acquire no glory from the performance. (Pythagoras.)

Integrity without knowledge is weak and useless, and knowledge without integrity is dangerous and dreadful. (Samuel Johnson.)

Let me be weighed in an even balance, that God may know mine integrity. (Job 31:6.)

Without integrity we have a weak foundation upon which to build other Christlike characteristics. (L. Lionel Kendrick, *Ensign*, November 1988, p. 23.)

Integrity is the value we set on ourselves. (James E. Faust, *Ensign*, May 1982, p. 47.)

The integrity of the upright shall guide them. (Proverbs 11:3.)

A person of integrity will assist others to be honest. (Marvin J. Ashton, *Ensign*, May 1982, p. 10.)

Performance of duty, regardless of the sacrifice involved, is a part of dealing justly with oneself and others. (James E. Faust, *Ensign*, May 1982, p. 48.)

It mattereth not whether the principle is popular or unpopular, I will always maintain a true principle, even if I stand alone in it. (Joseph Smith, *History of the Church*, 6:223.)

Jesus Christ

For behold, I am God; and I am a God of miracles; and I will show unto the world that I am the same yesterday, today, and forever. (2 Nephi 27:23.)

Nothing in all of human history equals the wonder, the splendor, the magnitude, or the fruits of the matchless life of the Son of God, who died for each of us. (Gordon B. Hinckley, *Ensign*, November 1984, p. 52.)

I am the first and the last; I am he who liveth, I am he who was slain; I am your advocate with the Father. (Doctrine and Covenants 110:4.)

No revelation that has ever taken place in society can be compared to that which has been produced by the words of Jesus Christ. (Mark Hopkins.)

Behold, Jesus Christ is the name which is given of the Father, and there is none other name given whereby man can be saved. (Doctrine and Covenants 18:23.)

Jesus is the Messiah, he is the Savior of the world. . . . Turn, twist, philosophize, mass sophistries as we will, this truth remains. (J. Reuben Clark, Jr., Conference Report, April 1934, p. 93.)

Christ is the verification of God's purposes for mankind, of the meaning of this life. (Neal A. Maxwell, *Ensign*, June 1984, p. 69.)

Knowledge

The heart of the prudent getteth knowledge; and the ear of the wise seeketh knowledge. (Proverbs 18:15.)

To be learned is good if they hearken unto the counsels of God. (2 Nephi 9:29.)

All wisdom, and all the arts and sciences in the world are from God, and are designed for the good of His people. (Brigham Young, *Journal of Discourses*, 13:147.)

Educate yourself not only for time, but also for eternity. (Joseph F. Smith, *Gospel Doctrine*, p. 269.)

The mere stuffing of the mind with a knowledge of facts is not education. (Joseph F. Smith, *Gospel Doctrine*, p. 269.)

And wisdom and knowledge shall be the stability of thy times, and strength of salvation: the fear of the Lord is his treasure. (Isaiah 33:6.)

Reading is to the mind what exercise is to the body. (Sir Richard Steele.)

Knowledge is a treasure but practice is the key to it. (Proverb.)

Knowledge comes, but wisdom lingers. (Alfred, Lord Tennyson.)

What we desperately need is to recognize and acquire that quality which converts knowledge into wisdom. (Marion G. Romney, *Ensign*, July 1983, p. 5.)

To be conscious that you are ignorant is a great step to knowledge. (Benjamin Disraeli.)

And if a person gains more knowledge and intelligence in this life through his diligence and obedience than another, he will have so much the advantage in the world to come. (Doctrine and Covenants 130:19.)

Laws

We believe in being subject to kings, presidents, rulers, and magistrates, in obeying, honoring, and sustaining the law. (Articles of Faith 1:12.)

Laws are to help us gain control so that we can have freedoms. (Anita Canfield, *The Young Woman and Her Self-Esteem*, p. 13.)

We believe that governments were instituted of God for the benefit of man; and that he holds men accountable for their acts . . . both in making laws and administering them, for the good and safety of society. (Doctrine and Covenants 134:1.)

Laws place the safety of all before the safety of individuals. (Marcus Cicero.)

Receive, I pray thee, the law from his mouth, and lay up his words in thine heart. (Job 22:22.)

Good laws make it easier to do right and harder to do wrong. (William E. Gladstone.)

For all who will have a blessing at my hands shall abide the law which was appointed for that blessing. (Doctrine and Covenants 132:5.)

The inadequacies of the laws of man provide no license for transgression under the laws of God. (Dallin H. Oaks, *Ensign*, November 1986, p. 20.)

The law also maketh you free. (Doctrine and Covenants 98:8.)

Leadership

Wherefore, be faithful; stand in the office which I have appointed unto you; succor the weak, lift up the hands which hang down, and strengthen the feeble knees. (Doctrine and Covenants 81:5.)

The upholding of the leadership of the kingdom of God arises out of the truth that our leaders . . . are the Lord's representatives. (Roy W. Doxey, *The Doctrine and Covenants Speaks,* 1:82.)

In leaders undue impatience and a gloomy mind are almost unpardonable, and it sometimes takes almost as much courage to wait as to act. (Joseph F. Smith, *Gospel Doctrine,* p. 156.)

Reason and calm judgment, these qualities especially belong to a leader. (Cornelius Tacitus.)

It is the task of leaders to match those talents with needs, and then to offer a challenge. (Gordon B. Hinckley, *Ensign,* November 1982, p. 8.)

> Most men can be led, but few can be driv'n
> In shunning perdition and striving for heav'n.
> (William Willes, *Hymns,* no. 244.)

It is necessary that he who commands well should have at some time obeyed. (Marcus Cicero.)

Let every man learn his duty, and to act in the office in which he is appointed, in all diligence. . . . He that learns not his duty and shows himself not approved shall not be counted worthy to stand. (Doctrine and Covenants 107:99–100.)

If you cannot keep your own counsel, how can you expect another person to keep it? (Proverb.)

And we did magnify our office unto the Lord, taking upon us the responsibility, answering the sins of the people upon our own heads if we did not teach them the word of God with all diligence. (Jacob 1:19.)

When seeking wise counsel, turn to those who have exhibited obedience to the commandments and willingness to follow the promptings of the Spirit. (Robert D. Hales, *Ensign*, November 1988, p. 10.)

When we are performing the Lord's work, we must do it the Lord's way. (Gene R. Cook, *Ensign*, May 1976, p. 104.)

Life

Behold, the Lord hath created the earth that it should be inhabited; and he hath created his children that they should possess it. (1 Nephi 17:36.)

> Our birth is but a sleep and a forgetting:
> The soul that rises with us, our life's star,
> Hath had elsewhere its setting,
> And cometh from afar.
> (William Wordsworth, *Ode: Intimations of Immortality.*)

You and I . . . were among those who passed that first test. . . . If we hadn't passed that test, we wouldn't be here with mortal bodies. (Harold B. Lee, *Relief Society Personal Study Guide*, 1988, p. 240.)

Remarkable as your body is, its prime purpose is even of greater importance—to serve as tenement for your spirit. (Russell M. Nelson, *Relief Society Personal Study Guide*, 1988, p. 248.)

Therefore this life became a probationary state; a time to prepare to meet God; a time to prepare for that endless state. (Alma 12:24.)

We are here in mortality, and the only way to go is through; there isn't any around! (Neal A. Maxwell, *Ensign*, May 1988, p. 9.)

Life is a school and not a reward. (Elaine Cannon, *Heart to Heart*, p. 52.)

God asks no man whether he will accept life. That is not the choice. You must take it. The only choice is how. (Henry Ward Beecher.)

We are pilgrims upon this earth, sent here with a mission to perform, a great work to do, for which we need guidance from the Lord. (Spencer W. Kimball, *Ensign*, July 1985, p. 4.)

Life is a voyage that's homeward bound. (Herman Melville.)

Love

Definition: "An intense fondness or deep devotion." (*Webster's New World Dictionary of the American Language*, p. 869.)

See that ye love one another with a pure heart fervently. (1 Peter 1:22.)

Riches take wings, comforts vanish, hope withers away, but love stays with us. (Lew Wallace.)

Someone has written, "Love is a verb." It requires doing — not just saying and thinking. (David B. Haight, *Ensign*, November 1982, p. 12.)

But charity is the pure love of Christ, and it endureth forever; and whoso is found possessed of it at the last day, it shall be well with him. (Moroni 7:47.)

The best investment I know of is charity: you get your principal back immediately, and draw a dividend every time you think of it. (Josh Billings.)

By this shall all men know that ye are my disciples, if ye have love one to another. (John 13:35.)

If we don't love ourselves, it's impossible to show much love for anybody else. (Terry R. Baker, *Ensign*, July 1984, p. 19.)

If you would be loved, love and be lovable. (Benjamin Franklin.)

Among the tragedies we see around us every day are the countless children and adults who are literally starving because they are not being fed a daily portion of love. (H. Burke Peterson, *Ensign*, May 1977, p. 68.)

Love is to give and to take at the right time in the right way. (Elaine Cannon, *Heart to Heart*, p. 63.)

And so love . . . cannot be expected to last forever unless it is continually fed with portions of love, the manifestation of esteem and admiration, the expressions of gratitude, and the consideration of unselfishness. (Spencer W. Kimball, *Marriage and Divorce*, p. 23.)

Marriage

Husbands, love your wives, even as Christ also loved the church, and gave himself for it. (Ephesians 5:25.)

God not only commends but he commands marriage. (Joseph F. Smith, *Gospel Doctrine*, p. 274.)

The decision to marry should be a happy, productive one—not one made by default in an attempt to escape a discontented, undirected life. (Karen Lynn Davidson, *Ensign*, June 1986, p. 52.)

Success in marriage depends not so much on finding the right person as it does on being the right person. (Lowell L. Bennion, *Looking Towards Marriage*, p. 47.)

Marriage is the closest and most intimate relationship one makes in this life, and the most serious and sacred decision. (Marion D. Hanks, *Ensign*, November 1984, p. 38.)

Marriage is the preserver of the human race. (Joseph F. Smith, *Gospel Doctrine*, p. 272.)

Latter-day revelation tells us that marriage under the law of the gospel and the holy priesthood is for eternity. (LDS Bible Dictionary, p. 729.)

True marriage is based on happiness . . . that comes from giving, serving, sharing, sacrificing, and selflessness. (Spencer W. Kimball, *Relief Society Course of Study*, 1987, p. 122.)

Missionaries

Definition of the word *mission:* "A sending out or being sent out with authority to perform a special duty." (*Webster's New World Dictionary of the American Language*, p. 942.)

For the fulness of mine intent is that I may persuade men to come unto the God of Abraham, and the God of Isaac, and the God of Jacob, and be saved. (1 Nephi 6:4.)

But when shall I be prepared to go there? Not while I have in my heart the love of this world more than the love of God. (Joseph F. Smith, *Millennial Star*, 56:385.)

I have always felt the best way to show love to others is to share the gospel with them. (Martha Cummings Kern, *Church News*, 2 Dec. 1978, p. 5.)

Behold, I, even I, will both search my sheep, and seek them out. (Ezekiel 34:11.)

> Let these, thy servants, speak
> With heart and voice of youth,
> And fill the world's dark lamps
> With light, the flame of truth.
> (Marilyn McMeen Brown, *Hymns*, no. 261.)

For though I preach the gospel, I have nothing to glory of: for necessity is laid upon me; yea, woe is unto me, if I preach not the gospel! (1 Corinthians 9:16.)

Let [a man] stand up full of the Holy Ghost, full of the power of God, and though he may use words and sentences in an awkward style, he will convince and convert more . . . than can the most polished orator destitute of the Holy Ghost. (Brigham Young, *Journal of Discourses*, 4:21.)

[Missionaries] were told to go trusting in the name of the Lord, and He would take care of them and go before them, and that his Spirit should go with them and His angels accompany them. (John Taylor, *Journal of Discourses*, 14:189.)

Those who fulfill an honorable mission develop an understanding of the gospel and a self-discipline that results in dedication and commitment to what they know to be true. (Royden G. Derrick, *Ensign*, May 1983, p. 25.)

And this gospel of the kingdom shall be preached in all the world for a witness unto all nations; and then shall the end come. (Matthew 24:14.)

If the question is asked, "You mean you are out to convert the entire world?" the answer is, "Yes. We will try to reach every living soul." (M. Russell Ballard, *Ensign*, November 1984, p. 15.)

Morality

Purify your hearts, and cleanse your hands and your feet before me, that I may make you clean. (Doctrine and Covenants 88:74.)

Old values are not upheld by the Church because they are old, but rather because through the ages they have proved to be right and because God has thus spoken. (Spencer W. Kimball, *Ensign*, November 1978, p. 105.)

Walk in the Spirit, and ye shall not fulfill the lust of the flesh. (Galatians 5:16.)

To educate a man in mind and not in morals is to educate a menace to society. (Theodore Roosevelt.)

Crowds cannot make right what God has declared to be wrong. (Neal A. Maxwell, *Ensign*, November 1988, p. 33.)

And ye must practise virtue and holiness before me continually. (Doctrine and Covenants 46:33.)

The surest step toward joy in the morning is virtue in the evening! (Russell M. Nelson, *Ensign*, November 1986, p. 67.)

He who is disposed to shun virtue lacks appreciation of life, its purposes, and the happiness and well-being of others. (Gordon B. Hinckley, *Ensign*, August 1988, p. 4.)

There was never yet a truly great man that was not at the same time virtuous. (Benjamin Franklin.)

Recommend to your children virtue; that alone can make happiness, not gold. (Ludwig van Beethoven.)

The family is the most effective place to instill lasting values in its members. (Ezra Taft Benson, *Ensign*, November 1982, p. 59.)

He that hath clean hands, and a pure heart. . . . He shall receive the blessing from the Lord. (Psalm 24:4–5.)

Mothers

Her ways are ways of pleasantness, and all her paths are peace. (Proverbs 3:17.)

The Lord holds motherhood and mothers sacred and in the highest esteem. (Spencer W. Kimball, *Ensign*, November 1978, p. 105.)

The future destiny of the child is always the work of the mother. (Napoleon Bonaparte.)

However potent she may be in matters extraneous to the home, she has no higher, loftier, and more divinely given calling and obligation than to be the right kind of wife and mother in her home. (Dean L. Larsen, *Ensign*, September 1982, p. 11.)

The mother's heart is the child's schoolroom. (Henry Ward Beecher.)

Men are what their mothers make them. (Ralph Waldo Emerson.)

Now they never had fought, yet they did not fear death; . . . they had been taught by their mothers, that if they did not doubt, God would deliver them. (Alma 56:47.)

Your mothers and grandmothers have sung a song that expressed the highest love and the noblest of womanly feelings. They have been nurturers and teachers. (James E. Faust, *Relief Society Course of Study*, 1987, p. 77.)

The real religion of the world comes . . . from mothers most of all, who carry the key of our souls in their bosoms. (Oliver Wendell Holmes.)

He maketh the barren woman to keep house, and to be a joyful mother of children. (Psalm 113:9.)

In her high duty and service to humanity in clothing eternal spirits with mortality, she is copartner with the Creator himself. (David O. McKay, *Relief Society Courses of Study*, 1985, p. 92.)

Obedience

And when we obtain any blessing from God, it is by obedience to that law upon which it is predicated. (Doctrine and Covenants 130:21.)

Obedience . . . shows self-control, strength of character. (Boy Scouts of America, *Handbook for Boys*, p. 35.)

The submissive soul will be led aright, enduring some things well while being anxiously engaged in setting other things right. (Neal A. Maxwell, *Ensign*, May 1985, p. 71.)

But seek ye first the kingdom of God, and his righteousness; and all these things shall be added unto you. (Matthew 6:33.)

Obedience to the law of Christ . . . is freedom of the soul. (Marion G. Romney, *Ensign*, November 1981, p. 45.)

The laws of obedience and sacrifice are indelibly intertwined. (Russell M. Nelson, *Ensign*, November 1987, p. 88.)

You cannot be a true man until you learn to obey. (Robert E. Lee.)

He that has learned to obey will know how to command. (Solon.)

How is it possible to expect mankind to take advice when they will not so much as take warning? (Jonathan Swift.)

Wicked men obey from fear: good men, from love. (Aristotle.)

I made this my rule: *When the Lord commands, do it.* (Joseph Smith, *History of the Church*, 2:170.)

If ye keep my commandments, ye shall abide in my love. (John 15:10.)

Obscenity

Definition: "[Something] offensive to modesty or decency, as language, conduct, a remark, an expression, or an act." (*Webster's New World Dictionary of the American Language*, p. 1013.)

Thou shalt not take the name of the Lord thy God in vain; for the Lord will not hold him guiltless that taketh his name in vain. (Exodus 20:7.)

Swearing is a vice that bespeaks a low standard of breeding. Blasphemous exclamations drive out all spirit of reverence. (David O. McKay, *Gospel Ideals*, p. 420.)

Despite all his refinement, the light and habitual taking of God's name in vain betrays a coarse and brutal will. (Edwin Chapin.)

But above all things, my brethren, swear not, neither by heaven, neither by the earth, neither by any other oath: but let your yea be yea; and your nay, nay; lest ye fall into condemnation. (James 5:12.)

To swear is neither brave, polite, nor wise. (Alexander Pope.)

Profanity is filthiness. A person is known as much by his language as he is by the company he keeps. (Joseph Fielding Smith, *Doctrines of Salvation*, 1:13.)

Isn't language pollution increasing because we are too eager to follow what others tell us is fashionable? (Anya Bateman, *Reader's Digest*, February 1989, p. 98.)

Profanity is profoundly offensive to those who worship the God whose name is desecrated. (Dallin H. Oaks, *Ensign*, May 1986, p. 51.)

Now my son, I would that ye should repent and forsake your sins, and go no more after the lusts of your eyes, . . . for except ye do this ye can in nowise inherit the kingdom of God. (Alma 39:9.)

Sins spawned by pornography unfortunately perpetuate other serious transgressions. (Spencer W. Kimball, *Ensign*, November 1976, p. 6.)

Nearly always, those who lose their virtue first partake of those things that excite passions within them or lower their resistance and becloud their minds. (Heber J. Grant, *Gospel Standards*, p. 55.)

But I say unto you, That whosoever looketh on a woman to lust after her hath committed adultery with her already in his heart. (Matthew 5:28.)

Parents

Children, obey your parents in the Lord: for this is right. (Ephesians 6:1.)

There are two ways of spreading light: to be the candle or the mirror that reflects it. We parents can be both. (Spencer W. Kimball, Conference Report, Stockholm Sweden Area Conference 1974, p. 49.)

The first and most important inner quality you can instill in a child is *faith in God*. The first and most important action a child can learn is *obedience*. And the most powerful tool you have with which to teach a child is *love*. (L. Tom Perry, *Ensign*, May 1983, p. 77.)

But I have commanded you to bring up your children in light and truth. (Doctrine and Covenants 93:40.)

Since our children already possess virtuous character traits, our job is to help the child recognize them, allow them to grow, and keep them from being overlooked. (Sherrie Johnson, *Ensign*, July 1983, p. 23.)

And ye shall teach [God's laws to] your children, speaking of them when thou sittest in thine house, and when thou walkest by the way, when thou liest down, and when thou risest up. (Deuteronomy 11:19.)

Train up a child in the way he should go—and walk there yourself once in a while. (Josh Billings.)

How long has it been since you took your children, whatever their size, in your arms and told them that you love them and are glad that they can be yours forever? (Spencer W. Kimball, *Ensign*, November 1974, pp. 112–13.)

A successful parent is one who has loved, one who has sacrificed, and one who has cared for, taught, and ministered to the needs of a child. (Howard W. Hunter, *Ensign*, November 1983, p. 65.)

Patience

Definition: "The bearing of suffering, provocation, delay, tediousness, etc. with calmness and self-control." (*Webster's New World Dictionary of the American Language*, p. 1072.)

And again, if he [your enemy] shall smite you the third time, and ye bear it patiently, your reward shall be doubled unto you four-fold. (Doctrine and Covenants 98:26.)

Perhaps any of us could get along with perfect people. But our task is to get along with imperfect people. (Richard L. Evans, *Richard Evans' Quote Book*, p. 165.)

Let us run with patience the race that is set before us. (Hebrews 12:1.)

> In patience, then, let us possess
> Our souls till he appear.
> (Mary Ann Morton, *Hymns*, no. 14.)

He that can have patience can have what he will. (Benjamin Franklin.)

Patience and fortitude conquer all things. (Ralph Waldo Emerson.)

It is a precious gift to have the gift of patience. (George Q. Cannon, *Gospel Truth*, p. 156.)

Ye are not able to abide the presence of God now, neither the ministering of angels; wherefore, continue in patience until ye are perfected. (Doctrine and Covenants 67:13.)

Perfection

Therefore I would that ye should be perfect even as I, or your Father who is in heaven is perfect. (3 Nephi 12:48.)

Our own progress can be enhanced if we can look for solutions instead of being critical of those around us and blaming external conditions for our lack of progress. (Marvin J. Ashton, *Ensign*, May 1983, p. 32.)

Total perfection is not necessary now. Striving for it, working hard toward it is. (Anita Canfield, *The Young Woman and Her Self-Esteem*, p. 34.)

Purity of heart means perfection; and the perfect will not only see God but will have friendship with him. (Spencer W. Kimball, *The Miracle of Forgiveness*, p. 27.)

If we refrain from evil acts, we have clean hands. If we refrain from forbidden thoughts, we have pure hearts. Those who would ascend and stand in the ultimate holy place must have both. (Dallin H. Oaks, *Ensign*, June 1986, p. 66.)

Ye are not able to abide the presence of God now, neither the ministering of angels; wherefore, continue in patience until ye are perfected. (Doctrine and Covenants 67:13.)

The road to perfection is always under construction. (Anonymous.)

To become perfect is to become as Jesus Christ. (David G. Lefgren.)

It will take us ages to accomplish this end [perfection], for there will be greater progress beyond the grave. (Joseph Fielding Smith, *Doctrines of Salvation* 2:18.)

And above all things, clothe yourselves with the bond of charity, as with a mantle, which is the bond of perfectness and peace. (Doctrine and Covenants 88:125.)

Perseverance

Definition: "Continuing to do something in spite of difficulties and obstacles." (*Webster's New World Dictionary of the American Language*, p. 1091.)

If thou wilt do good, yea, and hold out faithful to the end, thou shalt be saved in the kingdom of God, which is the greatest of all the gifts of God. (Doctrine and Covenants 6:13.)

Remind yourself that striving can be more important than arriving. (Marvin J. Ashton, *Relief Society Course of Study*, 1987, p. 57.)

That which we persist in doing becomes easier; not that the nature of the thing has changed, but that our power to do has increased. (Ralph Waldo Emerson.)

Let us lay aside every weight, and the sin which doth so easily beset us, and let us run with patience the race that is set before us. (Hebrews 12:1.)

Great works are performed not by strength but by perseverance. (Samuel Johnson.)

Our greatest glory is not in never falling, but in rising every time we fall. (Confucius.)

Saints are sinners who keep on trying. (Robert Louis Stevenson.)

Things generally turn up for those who keep digging. (Marvin J. Ashton, *Ensign*, September 1982, p. 75.)

Perseverance is essential to us in learning and living the principles of the gospel and . . . it will determine our progress as we strive to reach exaltation. (Joseph B. Wirthlin, *Ensign*, November 1987, p. 10.)

I have fought a good fight, I have finished my course, I have kept the faith. (2 Timothy 4:7.)

Plan of Salvation

Now, if it had not been for the plan of redemption, which was laid from the foundation of the world, there could have been no resurrection of the dead. (Alma 12:25.)

We knew the plan. We desired it; we endured it. We defended it. We even fought for it! (Barbara W. Winder, *Ensign*, November 1986, p. 90.)

But God did call on men . . . (this being the plan of redemption which was laid) saying: If ye will repent, and harden not your hearts, then will I have mercy upon you, through mine Only Begotten Son. (Alma 12:33.)

You were foreordained to come to earth at a time when the fulness of the gospel was on the earth. (David B. Haight, *Ensign*, November 1986, p. 37.)

When life ends, we shall return to a situation patterned after our life here, only less limited, more glorious, [and with] more increased joys. (Spencer W. Kimball, *Ensign*, May 1974, p. 118.)

For behold, this is my work and my glory—to bring to pass the immortality and eternal life of man. (Moses 1:39.)

And now, behold, I say unto you: This is the plan of salvation unto men, through the blood of mine Only Begotten, who shall come in the meridian of time. (Moses 6:62.)

Potential

The humblest member of the Church, if he keeps the commandments of God . . . will obtain an exaltation just as much as any other man in the celestial kingdom. (George Albert Smith, Conference Report, October 1933, p. 25.)

Men were born to succeed, not to fail. (Henry David Thoreau.)

The powers of the Soul are commensurate with its needs. (Ralph Waldo Emerson.)

Each of us has great gifts, but many of us severely limit ourselves with negative attitudes about our potential. (Gene R. Cook, *Ensign*, March 1986, p. 78.)

> For of all sad words of tongue or pen,
> The saddest are these: "It might have been!"
> (John Greenleaf Whittier.)

No one became thoroughly bad in one step. (Juvenal.)

Circumstance does not make the man; it reveals him to himself. (James Allen.)

The man who makes no mistakes does not usually make anything. (Edward John Phelps.)

We should never be surprised if our children grow up to be like us. Therefore, we must take the time to be the kind of people we would like our children to be. (N. Eldon Tanner, *Seek Ye First the Kingdom of God*, p. 212.)

If you treat a man as he is, he will remain as he is, but if you treat him as if he were what he ought to be, and could be, he will become what he ought to be, and should be. (Goethe.)

Prayer

But . . . humble yourselves before the Lord, and call on his holy name, and watch and pray continually, that ye may not be tempted above that which ye can bear, and thus be led by the Holy Spirit. (Alma 13:28.)

You will find that those who wait till the Spirit bids them pray, will never pray much upon this earth. (Brigham Young, *Discourses of Brigham Young*, p. 44.)

Do not pray for easier lives. Pray to be stronger men! Do not pray for tasks equal to your power. Pray for power equal to your tasks. (Phillips Brooks.)

If we were granted *all* of our prayers, there would be no death, no illness, no war, no trials, or no things to fear. To accomplish this, there could be no freedom and the purposes of the earth would be destroyed. (Max B. Skousen, *How to Pray and Stay Awake*, p. 125.)

Call unto me, and I will answer thee, and shew thee great and mighty things, which thou knowest not. (Jeremiah 33:3.)

It is the height of disloyalty to pray for God's will to be done and then fail to conform our lives to that will. (David O. McKay, *Secrets of a Happy Life*, p. 114.)

Draw near unto me and I will draw near unto you; seek me diligently and ye shall find me; ask, and ye shall receive; knock, and it shall be opened unto you. (Doctrine and Covenants 88:63.)

There are times when the only way the strait and narrow path can be followed is on one's knees! (Neal A. Maxwell, *Ensign*, May 1982, p. 38.)

The first and most fundamental virtue in effective prayer is faith. (David O. McKay, *Relief Society Course of Study*, 1987, p. 81.)

There is one part of prayer—the answer part—that perhaps, by comparison, we neglect. (Boyd K. Packer, *Ensign*, November 1979, p. 19.)

More things are wrought by prayer than this world dreams of. (Alfred, Lord Tennyson, *The Passing of Arthur*, line 415.)

But behold, I say unto you that ye must pray always, and not faint; that ye must not perform any thing unto the Lord save in the first place ye shall pray unto the Father in the name of Christ, that he will consecrate thy performance unto thee, that thy performance may be for the welfare of thy soul. (2 Nephi 32:9.)

Pride

Definition: "A justified or excessive belief in one's own worth, merit, superiority, etc." (*Webster's New World Dictionary of the American Language*, p. 1156.)

Woe unto them that are wise in their own eyes, and prudent in their own sight! (Isaiah 5:21.)

O the wise, and the learned, and the rich, that are puffed up in the pride of their hearts, and all those who preach false doctrines, . . . for they shall be thrust down to hell! (2 Nephi 28:15.)

Pride is a kind of pleasure produced by a man thinking too well of himself. (Baruch Spinoza.)

He that falls in love with himself will have no rivals. (Benjamin Franklin.)

O that ye would listen unto the word of his commands, and let not this pride of your hearts destroy your souls! (Jacob 2:16.)

Pride is a "my will" rather than "thy will" approach to life. (Ezra Taft Benson, *Ensign*, May 1986, p. 6.)

Many of us try to serve the Lord for purely selfish reasons. That is, we accept positions and take an active part so that we may stand in pride before our associates. (Max B. Skousen, *How to Pray and Stay Awake*, pp. 46–47.)

Was it not through pride that the devil became the devil? (Ezra Taft Benson, *Ensign*, May 1986, p. 6.)

Behold, are ye stripped of pride? I say unto you, if ye are not ye are not prepared to meet God. (Alma 5:28.)

Priesthood

The rights of the priesthood are inseparably connected with the powers of heaven, and . . . the powers of heaven cannot be controlled nor handled only upon the principles of righteousness. (Doctrine and Covenants 121:36.)

We can only exercise it [the priesthood] within the limits the Lord has set, upon the conditions he has specified, and in his name. (Marion G. Romney, *Ensign*, May 1982, p. 43.)

I would say that this Priesthood is not for the honor of man . . . but it is imparted to man in order that he may be made the medium of salvation to others. (John Taylor, *Journal of Discourses*, 24:35.)

If all priesthood bearers could catch the vision of the purposes of quorums and more fully understand the importance of priesthood work, the work would go forward with leaps and bounds. (Joseph B. Wirthlin, *Ensign*, August 1984, p. 13.)

Let us be active participants — not mere spectators — on the stage of priesthood power. (Thomas S. Monson, *Ensign*, November 1986, p. 42.)

As a preparatory priesthood it [the Aaronic Priesthood] is preparing you ultimately . . . for eternal life and exaltation. (Victor L. Brown, *Ensign*, November 1984, p. 39.)

The Melchizedek Priesthood holds the right of presidency, and has power and authority over all the offices in the church in all ages of the world, to administer in spiritual things. (Doctrine and Covenants 107:8.)

The Melchizedek Priesthood . . . is the power and authority to do all that is necessary to save and exalt the children of men. (Bruce R. McConkie, *Ensign*, May 1982, p. 33.)

Fathers benefit greatly from being trained in how to fulfill their family responsibilities, and the Melchizedek Priesthood quorum has the responsibility to see that they receive that training. (Joseph B. Wirthlin, *Ensign*, August 1984, p. 11.)

Following the priesthood of the Church is an expression of faith in the Lord's continuing guidance of his Church. (James E. Faust, *Relief Society Course of Study*, 1987, p. 79.)

> Brethren, pow'r by earthly standards
> Comes by rank or wealth or sword;
> But the pow'r above all others
> Is the priesthood of our Lord.
> (John Craven, *Hymns*, no. 320.)

[The] priesthood continueth in the church of God in all generations, and is without beginning of days or end of years. (Doctrine and Covenants 84:17.)

Procrastination

I made haste, and delayed not to keep thy commandments. (Psalm 119:60.)

Joshua didn't say choose you next year whom you will serve. (Neal A. Maxwell, *Ensign*, November 1974, p. 13.)

Procrastination is telling the Lord: "I'm not interested today." (Robert G. Allen.)

Procrastination is the thief of time. (Edward Young.)

Procrastination, as it may be applied to gospel principles, is the thief of eternal life. (Joseph Fielding Smith, *Improvement Era*, June 1969, p. 37.)

Never leave that till tomorrow which you can do today. (Benjamin Franklin.)

But behold, your days of probation are past; ye have procrastinated the day of your salvation. (Helaman 13:38.)

Repentance

Definition of the word *repent:* "To feel so contrite over one's sins as to change, or decide to change, one's ways." (*Webster's New World Dictionary of the American Language*, p. 1234.)

Sometimes we are afraid to repent because we condemn ourselves instead of condemning the sin. (Anita Canfield, *The Young Woman and Her Self-Esteem*, p. 65.)

Learn true doctrine—repentance *and* forgiveness; lay that burden of guilt down! (Boyd K. Packer, *Ensign*, November 1986, p. 18.)

I say unto you, that likewise joy shall be in heaven over one sinner that repenteth, more than over ninety and nine just persons, which need no repentance. (Luke 15:7.)

When a person repents, remorse of conscience brings the urge to abandon the sin and seek the Lord's forgiveness. (Roy W. Doxey, *The Doctrine and Covenants Speaks*, 1:502.)

Therefore, whosoever repenteth, and hardeneth not his heart, he shall have claim on mercy through mine Only Begotten Son, unto a remission of his sins; and these shall enter into my rest. (Alma 12:34.)

And when mistakes occur, let them become instructive, not destructive. (Neal A. Maxwell, *Ensign*, May 1982, p. 39.)

Growth comes of correction. Strength comes of repentance. (Gordon B. Hinckley, as quoted by Dallin H. Oaks, *Ensign*, February 1987, p. 68.)

To know ourselves diseased is half our cure. (Alexander Pope.)

Repentance is not an announcement. It is improved conduct. (Marvin J. Ashton, *Ensign*, September 1982, p. 75.)

One must repent and pray until doubt and darkness disappear and important things can be seen again. (F. Burton Howard, *Ensign*, November 1986, p. 77.)

Repentance is a change of behavior which invites forgiveness. (Theodore M. Burton, *Ensign*, May 1983, p. 70.)

Do not procrastinate the day of your repentance until the end; for after this day of life, which is given us to prepare for eternity, . . . cometh the night of darkness wherein there can be no labor performed. (Alma 34:33.)

Reverence

Definition: "A feeling of profound awe and respect." (*The American Heritage Dictionary*, p. 604.)

Reverence is the soul of true religion. (Marion G. Romney, *Ensign*, July 1983, p. 5.)

Let us have grace, whereby we may serve God acceptably with reverence and godly fear. (Hebrews 12:28.)

You are reverent as you serve God in your everyday actions. (*Boy Scout Handbook*, 1968, p. 51.)

When the names of God the Father and his Son, Jesus Christ, are used with reverence and authority, they invoke a power beyond what mortal man can comprehend. (Dallin H. Oaks, *Ensign*, May 1986, p. 51.)

Let them learn first to shew piety at home, . . . for that is good and acceptable before God. (1 Timothy 5:4.)

There is a little plant called reverence in the corner of my soul's garden, which I love to have watered once a week. (Oliver Wendell Holmes.)

Ye shall keep my sabbaths, and reverence my sanctuary: I am the Lord. (Leviticus 19:30.)

> Earthly thoughts, be silent now,
> While with reverence we assemble
> And before his presence bow.
> (*Hymns*, no. 132.)

Sacrifice

Definition: "In the simplest sense . . . sacrifice means to do something holy or godlike." (*Relief Society Personal Study Guide*, 1988, p. 128.)

Gather my saints together unto me; those that have made a covenant with me by sacrifice. (Psalm 50:5.)

Some men are willing to die for their faith, but they are not willing to fully live for it. (Ezra Taft Benson, *Ensign*, December 1988, p. 2.)

Sacrifices were . . . an acknowledgment on the part of the individual of his duty toward God, and also a thankfulness . . . for his life and blessings upon the earth. (LDS Bible Dictionary, p. 766.)

If we wish the blessing, we must pay the price. (Gordon B. Hinckley, *Ensign*, November 1984, p. 90.)

And inasmuch as ye impart of your substance unto the poor, ye will do it unto me. (Doctrine and Covenants 42:31.)

We must be willing to sacrifice everything. . . . Then we shall have peace in this world. (Marion G. Romney, Conference Report, September 1949, pp. 43–44.)

Selflessness is a key to happiness and effectiveness. (Spencer W. Kimball, *Relief Society Course of Study*, 1987, p. 124.)

By selflessness we demonstrate our true relationship with the Savior. (William R. Bradford, *Ensign*, April 1983, p. 51.)

There can be no true worship without sacrifice, and there can be no true sacrifice without a cause. (Russell M. Nelson, *Ensign*, November 1984, p. 32.)

Offer up spiritual sacrifices, acceptable to God by Jesus Christ. (1 Peter 2:5.)

Scouting

But they that wait upon the Lord shall renew their strength; they shall mount up with wings as eagles. (Isaiah 40:31.)

There is no more significant work in this world than the preparation of boys to become men of capacity, of strength, of integrity, who are qualified to live productive and meaningful lives. (Gordon B. Hinckley, *Ensign*, April 1985, p. 76.)

Scouting is growing into responsible manhood, learning to be of service to others. (William Hillcourt, *The Official Boy Scout Handbook*, 1979, p. 9.)

[The Scout program] is truly a builder of character, not only in young men, but also in the men who provide the leadership. (Ezra Taft Benson, *Ensign*, April 1985, p. 77.)

The Scout Law is based upon the codes of old, but transformed into a positive, living ideal for the modern boy. (*Scoutmaster's Handbook*, 1960, p. 20.)

Scouting teaches boys how to live, not merely how to make a living. (Thomas S. Monson, *Ensign*, November 1982, p. 20.)

Men have explored the wisdom of ages to give you the program of Scouting. (Boy Scouts of America, *Revised Handbook for Boys*, 1943, p. 5.)

The boy who climbs the summit cannot only tell where he has been, but also view what lies ahead. (David E. Lefgren.)

When we think of our responsibilities toward boys, let us remember that our task is larger than ourselves, our influence more lasting than our lives. (Thomas S. Monson, *Ensign*, April 1985, p. 77.)

Scriptures

I did liken all scriptures unto us, that it might be for our profit and learning. (1 Nephi 19:23.)

The holy scriptures are for children, to fill their eager minds with sacred truth. They are for youth, to prepare them for the challenges of our fast-moving world. They are for the sisters. . . . They are for the brethren of the priesthood. (Thomas S. Monson, *Ensign,* December 1985, p. 48.)

The holy scriptures represent mankind's spiritual memory. (Neal A. Maxwell, *Ensign,* November 1986, p. 52.)

What you bring away from the Bible depends to some extent on what you carry to it. (Oliver Wendell Holmes.)

Advance no principle but what you can prove, for one scriptural proof is worth ten thousand opinions. (The Quorum of the Twelve, 1838, *History of the Church,* 3:396.)

And the Book of Mormon and the holy scriptures are given of me for your instruction. (Doctrine and Covenants 33:16.)

A knowledge of the Bible without a college course is more valuable than a college course without the Bible. (William Lyon Phelps.)

All scripture is given by inspiration of God, and is profitable . . . for instruction in righteousness. (2 Timothy 3:16.)

There shouldn't be—there mustn't be—one family in this Church that doesn't take the time to read from the scriptures every day. (H. Burke Peterson, *Ensign,* May 1975, pp. 53-54.)

We scramble to honor appointments with physicians, lawyers, and businessmen. Yet we think nothing of postponing interviews with Deity—postponing scripture study. (Carlos E. Asay, *Ensign*, November 1978, p. 53.)

Second Coming

Behold, the great day of the Lord is at hand. . . . Let us, therefore, as a church and a people, and as Latter-day Saints, offer unto the Lord an offering in righteousness. (Doctrine and Covenants 128:24.)

I believe that our Great Maker is preparing the world, in His own good time, to become one nation, speaking one language, and then armies and navies will be no longer required. (Ulysses Simpson Grant.)

For the day of the Lord of Hosts soon cometh upon all nations, yea, upon every one; yea, upon the proud and lofty, and upon every one who is lifted up, and he shall be brought low. (2 Nephi 12:12.)

There will be some steep climbs ahead, but our Lord and Savior Jesus Christ has covenanted and promised to climb with each of us every step of the way. (Ardeth G. Kapp, *Ensign*, November 1986, p. 89.)

Yes, Armageddon lies ahead. But so does Adam-ondi-Ahman! (Neal A. Maxwell, *Relief Society Course of Study*, 1987, p. 41.)

If you do your duty . . . we'll have the protection, and shall pass through the afflictions in peace and in safety. (Wilford Woodruff, *The Young Woman's Journal*, 5:513.)

Watch ye therefore, and pray always, that ye may be accounted worthy to escape all these things that shall come to pass. (Luke 21:36.)

Self-Mastery

The only conquests which are permanent, and leave no regrets, are our conquests over ourselves. (Napoleon Bonaparte.)

It is impossible to rise higher as leaders than we rise as individuals. (Sterling W. Sill, *Especially for Mormons*, 4:8.)

The greatest battles of life are fought out daily in the silent chambers of the soul. (David O. McKay, *Especially for Mormons*, 3:9.)

If you cannot keep your own counsel how can you expect another person to keep it? (Proverb.)

We must be master of our beings and control ourselves, and not be controlled by some habit or by someone else. (Ted E. Brewerton, *Ensign*, November 1986, p. 30.)

Self-control comes through obedience. (Anita Canfield, *The Young Woman and Her Self-Esteem*, p. 18.)

He is strong who conquers others; he who conquers himself is mighty. (Lao-tse.)

Enduring well is accomplished by personal discipline hour by hour and day by day, not by public declaration. (Marvin J. Ashton, *Ensign*, November 1984, p. 21.)

If they humble themselves before me, and have faith in me, then will I make weak things become strong unto them. (Ether 12:27.)

Watch ye and pray, lest ye enter into temptation. The spirit truly is ready, but the flesh is weak. (Mark 14:38.)

For the natural man is an enemy to God, . . . unless he yields to the enticings of the Holy Spirit, and putteth off the natural man and becometh a saint through the atonement of Christ the Lord. (Mosiah 3:19.)

Therefore I would that ye should be perfect even as I, or your Father who is in heaven is perfect. (3 Nephi 12:48.)

Service

And behold, I tell you these things that ye may learn wisdom; that ye may learn that when ye are in the service of your fellow beings ye are only in the service of your God. (Mosiah 2:17.)

Great women and men are always more anxious to serve than to have dominion. (Spencer W. Kimball, *Relief Society Courses of Study*, 1985, p. 9.)

Acts of service can be small or grandiose. But they all produce the same effect. (Suzanne L. Hansen, *Working and Winning with Kids*, p. 26.)

Service is the very fiber of which an exalted life in the celestial kingdom is made. (Marion G. Romney, *Ensign*, June 1984, p. 6.)

As you exercise your time and talents in service, your faith will grow and your doubts will wane. (Gordon B. Hinckley, *Ensign*, April 1983, p. 7.)

When we concern ourselves more with others, there is less time to be concerned with ourselves. (Spencer W. Kimball, *Ensign*, October 1985, p. 3.)

Man's greatest happiness comes from losing himself for the good of others. (David O. McKay, as quoted by N. Eldon Tanner, *Ensign*, January 1983, p. 4.)

Loving service anonymously given may be unknown to man— but the gift and the giver are known to God. (Thomas S. Monson, *Ensign*, May 1983, p. 57.)

We become significant individuals as we serve others. (Spencer W. Kimball, *Ensign*, December 1974, p. 2.)

For not the hearers of the law are just before God, but the doers of the law shall be justified. (Romans 2:13.)

Unless we lose ourselves in the service of others our lives are largely lived to no real purpose. (Gordon B. Hinckley, *Ensign*, August 1982, p. 3.)

Our own strength and capacity will be doubled when we help others endure. (Marvin J. Ashton, *Ensign*, November 1984, p. 22.)

There is no happiness in having or getting, but only in giving. (Henry Drummond.)

It's not your blue blood, your pedigree or your college degree. It's what you do with your life that counts. (Millard Fuller, *Time*, 16 January 1989, p. 12.)

Therefore, strengthen your brethren in all your conversation, in all your prayers, in all your exhortations, and in all your doings. (Doctrine and Covenants 108:7.)

Success

Success comes from faith and work and prayer and from constant righteous effort. (Spencer W. Kimball, *Ensign*, November 1978, p. 105.)

Success is to be measured not so much by the position that one has reached in life as by the obstacles which he has overcome while trying to succeed. (Booker T. Washington.)

The future belongs to those who prepare for it—and who work for it and live for it. (Ralph Waldo Emerson.)

Most people would succeed in small things if they were not troubled with great ambitions. (Henry Wadsworth Longfellow.)

The secret of success is constancy to purpose. (Benjamin Disraeli.)

The world knows nothing of its greatest men. (Sir Henry Taylor.)

As long as we exercise love, patience, and understanding, even when no progress is apparent, we are not failing. (Marvin J. Ashton, *Ensign*, November 1984, p. 21.)

Talent

Definition: "A native ability for a specific pursuit, and [the word] connotes either that it is or can be cultivated by the one possessing it." (*Webster's New World Dictionary of the American Language*, p. 1486.)

And I would exhort you, my beloved brethren, that ye remember that every good gift cometh of Christ. (Moroni 10:18.)

Talents constitute our ability to make contributions to the welfare of our fellow men. (Roy W. Doxey, *The Doctrine and Covenants Speaks*, 1:464.)

Perhaps one of your gifts in life is as simple and effortless as the giving of a smile or a kind word. (James E. Faust, *Relief Society Personal Study Guide*, 1988, p. 291.)

Hide not your talents, they for use were made. What's a sun-dial in the shade? (Benjamin Franklin.)

Natural abilities are like natural plants; they need pruning by study. (Francis Bacon.)

They can because they think they can. (Virgil.)

Neglect not the gift that is in thee. (1 Timothy 4:14.)

For of him unto whom much is given much is required. (Doctrine and Covenants 82:3.)

The full story of Mormonism has never yet been written nor painted nor sculpted nor stolen. It remains for inspired hearts and talented fingers *yet* to reveal themselves. (Spencer W. Kimball, *Ensign*, July 1977, p. 5.)

Teaching

Definition of the word *teach:* "To show how to do something; demonstrate; to provide with knowledge and insight." (*Webster's New World Dictionary of the American Language,* p. 1495.)

But ye will teach [your children] to walk in the ways of truth and soberness; ye will teach them to love one another, and to serve one another. (Mosiah 4:15.)

The secret of education lies in respecting the pupil. (Ralph Waldo Emerson.)

And as all have not faith, seek ye diligently and teach one another words of wisdom; yea, seek ye out of the best books words of wisdom; seek learning, even by study and also by faith. (Doctrine and Covenants 88:118.)

Effective teaching by the Spirit can stir the souls of men with a desire to live the principles of the gospel of Jesus Christ more completely. (M. Russell Ballard, *Ensign,* May 1983, pp. 68–69.)

To be successful as a teacher of youth, one must truly love each of them regardless of his activity. (Victor L. Brown, *Ensign,* May 1982, p. 35.)

And the Spirit shall be given unto you by the prayer of faith; and if ye receive not the Spirit ye shall not teach. (Doctrine and Covenants 42:14.)

What nobler employment, or more valuable to the state, than that of the man who instructs the rising generation? (Marcus Cicero.)

For it is not ye that speak, but the Spirit of your Father which speaketh in you. (Matthew 10:20.)

The best way of training the young is to train yourself at the same time; not to admonish them, but to be seen never doing that of which you would admonish them. (Plato.)

Yea, teach parents that they must repent and be baptized, and humble themselves as their little children, and they shall all be saved with their little children. (Moroni 8:10.)

Every human soul is teaching something to someone nearly every minute here in mortality. (M. Russell Ballard, *Ensign*, May 1983, p. 70.)

Temptation

Blessed is the man that resisteth temptation: for when he is tried, he shall receive the crown of life, which the Lord hath promised to them that love him. (JST, James 1:12.)

Temptations come to all people. The difference between the reprobate and the worthy person is generally that one yielded and the other resisted. (Spencer W. Kimball, *The Miracle of Forgiveness*, p. 86.)

He that is busy is tempted by but one devil; he that is idle, by a legion. (Thomas Fuller.)

Let no man say when he is tempted, I am tempted of God: for God cannot be tempted with evil, neither tempteth he any man. (James 1:13.)

Nothing is so good as it seems beforehand. (George Eliot.)

Submit yourselves therefore to God. Resist the devil, and he will flee from you. (James 4:7.)

The devil has no power over us only as we permit him. (Joseph Smith, *Teachings of the Prophet Joseph Smith*, p. 181.)

Behold, verily, verily, I say unto you, ye must watch and pray always lest ye enter into temptation; for Satan desireth to have you, that he may sift you as wheat. (3 Nephi 18:18.)

To remain clean and worthy, one must stay positively and conclusively away from the devil's territory, avoiding the least approach toward evil. Satan leaves his fingerprints. (Spencer W. Kimball, *The Miracle of Forgiveness*, p. 232.)

Testimony

My soul hath kept thy testimonies; and I love them exceedingly. (Psalms 119:167.)

As testimony fills my heart,
It dulls the pain of days.
(Loren C. Dunn, *Hymns*, no. 137.)

A testimony is one of the few possessions we may take with us when we leave this life. (Ezra Taft Benson, *Ensign*, May 1982, p. 62.)

The testimony that is earned is the only testimony that lasts. (Max B. Skousen, *How to Pray and Stay Awake*, p. 76.)

Be not thou therefore ashamed of the testimony of our Lord. (2 Timothy 1:8.)

A testimony is to be *found* in the *bearing* of it! (Boyd K. Packer, *Ensign*, January 1983, p. 54.)

Thus Satan thinketh to overpower your testimony in this generation, that the work may not come forth in this generation. (Doctrine and Covenants 10:33.)

When we *desire* to gain a testimony, *desire* to know, *desire* to believe, testimony can begin or grow. (John K. Carmack, *Ensign*, November 1988, p. 26.)

Not to be valiant in one's testimony is a tragedy of eternal consequences. (Ezra Taft Benson, *Ensign*, February 1987, p. 2.)

Thankfulness

And he who receiveth all things with thankfulness shall be made glorious; and the things of this earth shall be added unto him, even an hundred fold, yea, more. (Doctrine and Covenants 78:19.)

Absence of gratitude is the mark of the narrow, uneducated mind. (Gordon B. Hinckley, *Ensign*, August 1988, p. 3.)

In every thing give thanks: for this is the will of God in Christ Jesus concerning you. (1 Thessalonians 5:18.)

We have been the recipients of the choicest bounties of heaven. . . . But we have forgotten God. We have forgotten the gracious hand which preserved us in peace. (Abraham Lincoln, as quoted in John Wesley Hill, *Abraham Lincoln, Man of God*, p. 391.)

Live in thanksgiving daily, for the many mercies and blessings which he doth bestow upon you. (Alma 34:38.)

He that enjoys aught without thanksgiving is as though he robbed God. (Chrysostom.)

Without appreciation, there is arrogance and evil. (Gordon B. Hinckley, *Ensign*, August 1988, p. 3.)

Let not your mind run on what you lack as much as on what you have already. (Marcus Aurelius.)

When thou risest in the morning let thy heart be full of thanks unto God; and if ye do these things, ye shall be lifted up at the last day. (Alma 37:37.)

Thoughts

For as he thinketh in his heart, so is he. (Proverbs 23:7.)

They are never alone that are accompanied with noble thoughts. (Sir Philip Sidney.)

Nurture your mind with great thoughts. (Benjamin Disraeli.)

Crimes are not committed in deed until they have been committed in thought. (John Lubbock.)

Thinking is like loving and dying. Each of us must do it for himself. (Josiah Royce.)

Our minds have unbelievable power over our bodies. (André Maurois.)

Thoughts lead to acts, acts lead to habits, habits lead to character—and our character will determine our eternal destiny. (Ezra Taft Benson, *Relief Society Course of Study,* 1987, p. 131.)

All that we are is the result of what we have thought. What we think, we become. (Buddha.)

I will be, when my life's labor is complete, the product of my thoughts. (George Albert Smith, *Sharing the Gospel with Others,* p. 63.)

If thoughts make us what we are, and we are to be like Christ, then we must think Christlike thoughts. (Ezra Taft Benson, *Relief Society Course of Study,* 1987, p. 133.)

Look unto me in every thought. (Doctrine and Covenants 6:36.)

Tithing

Bring ye all the tithes into the storehouse, that there may be meat in mine house, and prove me now herewith, saith the Lord of hosts, if I will not open you the windows of heaven and pour you out a blessing, that there shall not be room enough to receive it. (Malachi 3:10.)

The law of tithing is a test by which the people as individuals shall be proved. (Joseph F. Smith, *Gospel Doctrine*, p. 226.)

Our tithing, our labor, our works are not for the exaltation of the Almighty, but they are for us. (Wilford Woodruff, as quoted in *Profiles of the Presidents*, p. 155.)

The Lord will open the windows of heaven according to our need, and not according to our greed. (Gordon B. Hinckley, *Ensign*, May 1982, p. 40.)

Tithing is, however, a voluntary offering because the Lord does not compel his people to live a commandment. . . . Each person decides whether or not he wants the blessing arising from obedience to the law. (Roy W. Doxey, *The Doctrine and Covenants Speaks*, 2:351.)

Will a man rob God? Yet ye have robbed me. But ye say: Wherein have we robbed thee? In tithes and offerings. (3 Nephi 24:8.)

To fail to meet this obligation [tithing] in full is to omit a weighty matter. (Spencer W. Kimball, *Ensign*, November 1980, p. 78.)

Those who have thus been tithed shall pay one-tenth of all their interest annually; and this shall be a standing law unto them forever. (Doctrine and Covenants 119:4.)

The man who rejects the law of the tithe is the man who has not given it a fair try. (Howard W. Hunter, Conference Report, April 1964, p. 35.)

And of all that thou shalt give me I will surely give the tenth unto thee. (Genesis 28:22.)

Transgression

Definition of the word *transgress:* "To act in violation of a law or commandment." (*The American Heritage Dictionary*, p. 733.)

And now, I say unto you . . . that after ye have known and have been taught all these things, if ye should transgress and go contrary to that which has been spoken, that ye do withdraw yourselves from the Spirit of the Lord, that it may have no place in you to guide you in wisdom's paths. (Mosiah 2:36.)

Hosts of capable souls have heedlessly put themselves into the enemy's power by yielding to the treacherous invitation to fraternize with sin. (James E. Talmage, *The Vitality of Mormonism*, p. 335.)

And now, because of stiffneckedness and unbelief they understood not my word. (3 Nephi 15:18.)

For rebellion is as the sin of witchcraft, and stubbornness is as iniquity and idolatry. (1 Samuel 15:23.)

Beware of scars that disfigure, that have come to you in places where you ought not have gone, that have befallen you in unworthy undertakings; beware of the wounds of battle in which you have been fighting on the wrong side. (James E. Talmage, Conference Report, October 1913, p. 117.)

His own iniquities shall take the wicked himself, and he shall be holden with the cords of his sins. (Proverbs 5:22.)

Positive rejection of the truth is even graver than passive inattention or neglect. (James E. Talmage, *Vitality of Mormonism*, pp. 280–281.)

Sin . . . is service to Satan. (Spencer W. Kimball, *The Miracle of Forgiveness*, p. 20.)

Break off thy sins by righteousness, and thine iniquities by shewing mercy to the poor. (Daniel 4:27.)

Truth

A true witness delivereth souls: but a deceitful witness speaketh lies. (Proverbs 14:25.)

No legacy is so rich as honesty. (William Shakespeare.)

These, then, are the steps on the way to truth: Desire, prayer, study, and practice. They form the eternal price which must be paid for truth. (John A. Widtsoe, *Evidences and Reconciliations*, 3:84.)

Sanctify them through thy truth. (John 17:17.)

So near is falsehood to truth that a wise man would do well not to trust himself on the narrow edge. (Marcus Cicero.)

In some instances, the merciful companion to truth is *silence*. Some truths are best left unsaid. (Russell M. Nelson, as quoted by Dallin H. Oaks, *Ensign*, February 1987, p. 69.)

If you tell the truth you don't have to remember anything. (Mark Twain.)

Men make constitutions and enact laws . . . but the fundamental laws of truth are eternal; they will never be amended, they will never be changed. (James E. Talmage, Conference Report, October 1918, pp. 60–61.)

He that doeth truth cometh to the light. (John 3:21.)

Womanhood

To be a righteous woman during the winding up scenes on this earth, before the second coming of our Savior, is an especially noble calling. (Spencer W. Kimball, *Ensign*, November 1978, p. 103.)

Great women respond generously to their instincts to do good. (James E. Faust, *Ensign*, September 1986, p. 20.)

There is in every true woman's heart a spear of heavenly fire. (Washington Irving.)

> The errand of angels is given to women;
> And this is a gift that, as sisters, we claim:
> To do whatsoever is gentle and human,
> To cheer and to bless in humanity's name.
> (Emily H. Woodmansee, *Hymns*, no. 309.)

When you educate a man you educate an individual; when you educate a woman you educate a whole family. (R. M. MacIver.)

Into a woman's keeping is committed the destiny of the generations to come after us. (Theodore Roosevelt.)

> They [women] are the books, the arts, the academes,
> That show, contain, and nourish all the world.
> (William Shakespeare.)

A gracious woman retaineth honour. (Proverbs 11:16.)

One of the important messages that emerges from the history of great women in all ages is that they cared more for the future of their families than for their own comfort. (Spencer W. Kimball, *Ensign*, November 1978, p. 103.)

Word of Wisdom

And all the saints who remember to keep and do these sayings, walking in obedience to the commandments, shall receive health in their navel and marrow to their bones; and shall find wisdom and great treasures of knowledge, even hidden treasures. (Doctrine and Covenants 89:18, 19.)

The Word of Wisdom is spiritual. But the largest measure of good derived from its observance is in increased faith and the development of more spiritual power and wisdom. (Stephen L Richards, Conference Report, April 1949, p. 141.)

And it pleaseth God that he hath given all these things unto man; for unto this end were they made to be used, with judgment, not to excess, neither by extortion. (Doctrine and Covenants 59:20.)

Once we choose to use a habit-forming drug, we are bound to the consequences of that choice. (Russell M. Nelson, *Ensign*, November 1988, p. 7.)

If any man defile the temple of God, him shall God destroy; for the temple of God is holy, which temple ye are. (1 Corinthians 3:17.)

From trial comes a habit. From habit comes dependence. From dependence comes addiction. (Russell M. Nelson, *Ensign*, November 1988, p. 6.)

There is no more dangerous drug—and certainly none that has done more damage or wrecked more lives over the years—than alcohol. (Godfrey Sperling, Jr., *Deseret News*, 24 September 1986, p. A9.)

We give you warning that Satan and his emissaries will strive to entice you to use harmful substances, because they well know if you partake, your spiritual powers will be inhibited and you will be in their evil power. (Ezra Taft Benson, *Ensign*, May 1983, p. 55.)

Drink has brought more woe and misery, broken more hearts, wrecked more homes, committed more crimes, filled more coffins, than all the wars the world has suffered. (First Presidency, Conference Report, October 1942, p. 8.)

My experience through life has convinced me that abstinence from spirituous liquors is the best safe-guard to morals and health. (Robert E. Lee.)

I beseech you therefore, brethren, by the mercies of God, that ye present your bodies a living sacrifice, holy, acceptable unto God, which is your reasonable service. (Romans 12:1.)

Work

The sleep of a labouring man is sweet, whether he eat little or much: but the abundance of the rich will not suffer him to sleep. (Ecclesiastes 5:12.)

Work is something more than the final end result. It is a *discipline*. (L. Tom Perry, *Ensign*, November 1986, p. 63.)

It is better to wear out than to rust out. (Richard Cumberland.)

We were under the necessity of laboring with our hands, hiring out by day's work . . . and by continuous labor were enabled to get a comfortable maintenance. (Joseph Smith—History 1:55.)

In all labour there is profit. (Proverbs 14:23.)

> Count that day lost whose low descending sun
> Views from thy hand no worthy action done.
> (Anonymous.)

The best angle from which to approach a problem is the try-angle. (Anonymous.)

Every piece of work we do is a portrait of the one who produced it. (J. Richard Clarke, *Ensign*, May 1982, p. 78.)

Therefore, we preach the gospel of industry, the gospel of economy, the gospel of sobriety. (Joseph F. Smith, *Gospel Doctrine*, p. 208.)

Worldliness

Definition of the word *worldly:* "Devoted to or concerned with the affairs, pleasures, etc., of this world." (*Webster's New World Dictionary of the American Language,* p. 1685.)

But wo unto the rich, who are rich as to the things of the world. For because they are rich they despise the poor, and they persecute the meek, and their hearts are upon their treasures; wherefore, their treasure is their god. And behold, their treasure shall perish with them also. (2 Nephi 9:30.)

We must clearly understand that it is not safe to move in the same direction the world is moving, even though we remain slightly behind the pace they set. (Dean L. Larsen, *Ensign,* May 1983, p. 34.)

For what is a man profited, if he shall gain the whole world, and lose his own soul? or what shall a man give in exchange for his soul? (Matthew 16:26.)

Prosperity is only an instrument to be used, not a deity to be worshipped. (Calvin Coolidge.)

For to be carnally minded is death; but to be spiritually minded is life and peace. (Romans 8:6.)

Great men are they who see that spiritual [force] is stronger than any material force. (Ralph Waldo Emerson.)

Youth

Let no man despise thy youth; but be thou an example of the believers, in word, in conversation, in charity, in spirit, in faith, in purity. (1 Timothy 4:12.)

Reserved by the Lord for this time, they [the youth] must now be *preserved* by parents and *prepared* for their special moment in human history! They have been *held back* to come forth at this time, but now they need to be *pushed forward* to meet their rendezvous. (Neal A. Maxwell, *Ensign*, April 1985, p. 8.)

Learn wisdom in thy youth; yea, learn in thy youth to keep the commandments of God. (Alma 37:35.)

Consider what heavy responsibility lies upon you in your youth, to determine, among realities, by what you will be delighted, and, among imaginations, by whose you will be led. (John Ruskin.)

Freedom of choice places a great responsibility on young people. (Howard W. Hunter, *Youth of the Noble Birthright*, p. 101.)

I challenge the young women of the Church who associate with and date our young priesthood bearers to become real guardians of their morality. (David B. Haight, *Ensign*, November 1977, p. 56.)

Faithful Latter-day Saint young women can have a great impact for good in helping young men to magnify their priesthood. (Ezra Taft Benson, *Ensign*, November 1986, p. 83.)

How glorious and near to the angels is youth that is clean. (The First Presidency, as quoted by Harold B. Lee, *Stand Ye in Holy Places*, p. 376.)

Bibliography

Note: The four standard works, *History of the Church*, the *Improvement Era*, the *New Era*, the *Ensign*, Conference Reports, *Hymns*, and Relief Society courses of study are publications of The Church of Jesus Christ of Latter-day Saints.

The American Heritage Dictionary. New York: Dell Publishing Co., 1974.

Ballard, Melvin J. *The Three Degrees of Glory.* Salt Lake City: Joseph Lyon and Associates, 1925.

Bateman, Anya. "I'm Sick of the F Word." *Reader's Digest,* February 1989.

Bennion, Lowell L. *Looking Towards Marriage.* Salt Lake City: Deseret Book Company, 1972.

Benson, Ezra Taft. *To the Mothers in Zion* [pamphlet]. Salt Lake City: The Church of Jesus Christ of Latter-day Saints, 1987.

Boy Scouts Handbook. 7th ed. New Brunswick, New Jersey: Boy Scouts of America, 1968.

Canfield, Anita. *The Young Woman and Her Self-Esteem.* Salt Lake City: Randall Book, 1983.

Cannon, Elaine. *Heart to Heart.* Salt Lake City: Bookcraft, 1983.

Cannon, George Q. *Gospel Truth.* Salt Lake City: Deseret Book Co., 1987.

Carnegie, Dale. *How to Win Friends and Influence People.* New York: Pocket Books, 1971.

Cline, Victor B. *How to Make Your Child a Winner.* New York: Walker & Co., 1980.

Doxey, Roy W. *The Doctrine and Covenants Speaks.* 2 vols. Salt Lake City: Deseret Book Company, 1976.

Dunn, Paul H., and Richard M. Eyre. *The Birth That We Call Death.* Salt Lake City: Bookcraft, 1976.

Evans, Richard L. *Richard Evans' Quote Book.* Salt Lake City: Publishers Press, 1971.

Flexner, Stuart B. *Family Word Finder.* Pleasantville, N.Y.: Reader's Digest, 1986.

Fuller, Millard. "A Bootstrap Approach to Low-Cost Housing." *Time,* 16 January 1989.

Grant, Heber J. *Gospel Standards.* Compiled by G. Homer Durham. Salt Lake City: Improvement Era, 1944.

Handbook for Boys. New York: Boy Scouts of America, 1948.

Hansen, Suzanne Lindman. *Working and Winning with Kids.* Orem, Utah: Randall Book, 1983.

Hill, John Wesley. *Abraham Lincoln, Man of God.* 4th ed. New York: G. P. Putnam's Sons, 1927.

Hillcourt, William. *The Official Boy Scout Handbook.* 9th ed. Irving, Texas: Boy Scouts of America, 1979.

Hunter, Howard W. *Youth of the Noble Birthright.* Salt Lake City: Deseret Book Company, 1960.

Hyman, Robin. *The Quotation Dictionary.* New York: Collier Books, 1962.

Kimball, Spencer W. *Faith Precedes the Miracle.* Salt Lake City: Deseret Book Company, 1972.

———. *Marriage and Divorce.* Salt Lake City: Deseret Book Company, 1976.

———. *The Miracle of Forgiveness.* Salt Lake City: Bookcraft, 1969.

———. *The Teachings of Spencer W. Kimball.* Salt Lake City: Bookcraft, 1982.

———. *Tragedy or Destiny?* Salt Lake City: Deseret Book Company, 1977.

Lee, Harold B. *Stand Ye in Holy Places.* Salt Lake City: Deseret Book Company, 1974.

Maxwell, Neal A. *Of One Heart.* Salt Lake City: Deseret Book Company, 1975.

McConkie, Bruce R. *Doctrinal New Testament Commentary,* vol. 1. Salt Lake City: Bookcraft, 1965.

———. *The Mortal Messiah,* vol. 1. Salt Lake City: Deseret Book Company, March 1983.

McKay, David O. *Gospel Ideals.* Salt Lake City: Improvement Era, 1953.

———. *Secrets of a Happy Life.* Ed. Llewelyn R. McKay. Salt Lake City: Bookcraft, 1967.

———. *Treasures of Life.* Comp. Claire Middlemiss. Salt Lake City: Deseret Book Company, 1965.

Miller, Stanley, comp. *Especially for Mormons,* vol. 1. Provo, Utah: Kellirae Arts, 1971.

Miller, Stan and Sharon, comp. *Especially for Mormons,* vols. 2 and 3. Provo, Utah: Kellirae Arts, 1973, 1976.

Miller, Stan and Sharon, and Sherm and Peggy Fugal, comp. *Especially for Mormons,* vol. 4. Provo, Utah: Kellirae Arts, 1978.

Revised Handbook for Boys, 1st ed. New York: Boy Scouts of America, 1943.

Scoutmaster's Handbook, 5th ed. New Brunswick, New Jersey: Boy Scouts of America, 1960.

Skousen, Max B. *How to Pray and Stay Awake.* Salt Lake City: Bookcraft, 1949.

Smith, George Albert. *Sharing the Gospel with Others.* Salt Lake City: Deseret Book Company, 1948.

Smith, Joseph. *Teachings of the Prophet Joseph Smith.* Compiled by Joseph Fielding Smith. Salt Lake City: Deseret Book Company, 1977.

Smith, Joseph F. *Gospel Doctrine.* Salt Lake City: Deseret Book Company, 1977.

Smith, Joseph Fielding. *Doctrines of Salvation.* Compiled by Bruce R. McConkie. 3 vols. Salt Lake City: Bookcraft, 1954–56.

Sperling, Godfrey, Jr. *Deseret News,* 24 September 1986.

Talmage, James E. *Jesus the Christ.* Salt Lake City: Deseret Book Company, 1977.

———. *Vitality of Mormonism.* Boston, Mass.: Gotham Press, 1919.

Tanner, N. Eldon. *Seek Ye First the Kingdom of God.* Compiled by LaRue Sneff. Salt Lake City: Deseret Book Co., 1973.

Wallis, Charles L. *The Treasure Chest.* New York: Harper & Row, 1965.

Watson, Lillian Eichler. *Light from Many Lamps.* New York: Simon & Schuster, 1979.

Webster's Encyclopedic Dictionary. New York: Consolidated Book Publishers, 1971.

Webster's New World Dictionary of the American Language. New York: World Publishing Co., 1958.

West, Emerson Roy. *Profiles of the Presidents.* Salt Lake City: Deseret Book Company, 1972.

———. *Vital Quotations.* Salt Lake City: Bookcraft, 1968.

Widtsoe, John A. *Evidences and Reconciliations,* vol 3. Salt Lake City: Bookcraft, 1951.

Woman. Salt Lake City: Deseret Book Company, 1979.

Woodruff, Wilford. *Young Woman's Journal,* vol. 5. Salt Lake City: The Church of Jesus Christ of Latter-day Saints, 1894.

Young, Brigham. *Discourses of Brigham Young.* Compiled by John A. Widtsoe. Salt Lake City: Deseret Book Company, 1977.

Zimmerman, Gertrude, comp. *Webster's New World Dictionary of the American Language.* New York: World Publishing Company, 1958.